John Whitaker

The Genuine History of the Britons

Asserted in a full and candid refutation of Mr. Macpherson's Introduction to the

history of Great Britain and Ireland

John Whitaker

The Genuine History of the Britons
Asserted in a full and candid refutation of Mr. Macpherson's Introduction to the history of Great Britain and Ireland

ISBN/EAN: 9783337323172

Printed in Europe, USA, Canada, Australia, Japan

Cover: Foto ©ninafisch / pixelio.de

More available books at **www.hansebooks.com**

THE GENUINE HISTORY

OF THE

BRITONS

ASSERTED.

IN

A FULL AND CANDID REFUTATION

OF

MR. MACPHERSON'S INTRODUCTION

TO THE

HISTORY OF GREAT BRITAIN AND IRELAND.

By the Rev. Mr. WHITAKER,

AUTHOR OF

THE HISTORY OF MANCHESTER.

Sold by DODSLEY, Pall-Mall; PAYNE, Mews-gate; BAKER and LEIGH, York-Street, Covent-Garden; CADELL, Strand; WHITE, LOWNDES, Fleet-Street; DAVIS, Holborne; PARKER, FLETCHER, Oxford; and the MERRILS, Cambridge. M DCC LXXII.

THE GENUINE HISTORY

OF THE

BRITONS

ASSERTED.

CONTENTS.

INTRODUCTION, *p.* 1—9

THE NATURE AND TIME OF THE FIRST COLONY THAT CAME INTO BRITAIN, 11—32

THE NATURE AND TIME OF THE SECOND, 33—66

THE POSITION, MANNERS, AND TRANSACTIONS OF BOTH IN THE ISLAND, 66—105

THE DERIVATION OF THE IRISH FROM BOTH, 106—153

THE DERIVATION OF THE SCOTS FROM THE IRISH, 154—293

THE CONCLUSION, 295—304.

THE
GENUINE HISTORY
OF THE
BRITONS
ASSERTED.

TO an hiſtorian that is curious to obſerve the ſtriking variations of national characters, and to a philoſopher that is delighted to note the advancements of the human mind in ſentiment and knowledge, the great and recent change in the hiſtorical genius of Scotland muſt appear equally remarkable and pleaſing [1]. Accuſtomed as the Scotch have for ages been to believe implicitly in a fictitious and fantaſtical hiſtory, they have lately emancipated their minds from the bondage, and in a great meaſure

[1] Of Scotland, properly ſo called, or the country to the North of Forth and Clyde.

renounced

renounced the fabulous fyftem of their anceftors. The defpicable forgeries of their lying annalifts are now no longer obtruded upon us, by the zeal of miftaken patriotifm, for the truths and realities of hiftory. They are either brought forward with a diffidence that betrays its own convictions of their falfhood, are mentioned merely to be condemned, or are entirely paft over in a contemptuous filence. And that enlarged and mafculine turn of thinking, which commenced near two centuries ago in England, has happily extended its influence among the mountains of Scotland. The monftrous creations of a Geoffrey and a Fordun, or the authors that they plundered, the wild fpecters and goblins which had for ages hovered in the gloom of our earlier hiftory, are now chaced away by the daylight that is diffufed over the face of our annals. The Grecian and Roman writers are allowed to be the only ftandards of hiftorical truth. And the whole Ifland is now for the firft time united in the profecution of its genuine hiftory.

The human mind, however, even in its detection of the greateft falfities, is continually checked in its operations by the feeblenefs of its own efforts, and is perpetually ftopt in its progrefs by the contractednefs of its own views. Its views are generally limited to a fingle point. And its efforts are generally too weak, even when they have triumphed over fome of its

own

own prejudices, to counteract the full force of national vanity, and to suppress the whole power of hereditary credulity, in itself or in others. Ireland remains to this day superstitiously devoted to her ancient history, sullenly turns away from the light of reformation that is spread over the neighbouring island, and wraps herself in the gloom of her own legendary annals. And the genius of Scotland has so greatly vitiated her judgement by the long indulgence of her fancy in history, that even now, when she is reclaimed from her former extravagancies, she seems strongly inclined to wanton excursions in the regions of fact and incident. That national vanity which originally generated, and afterwards supported, the mis-shapen brood of her former fictions, appears equally active at present among the historical writers of Scotland, and has equally a tendency to distort and disguise the genuine history of our island. And this is particularly obvious in the repeated attempts that have been recently made by them, to new-model the ancient accounts of Ireland and the Scotch, and to fashion them to the fantastic standard of their own popular caprices. The ancient historians speak of Ireland as the mother of the Scots, and Caledonia as the parent of the Picts: and the present Scotch must therefore be the descendants of Irish emigrants, who settled amongst the Caledonians, and communicated their own name to them. But this, it seems,

seems, the Scotch difdain to admit. And in that spirit of humourfome pride, which had originally loaded the hiftory of their country with all the impertinence of dreams, the whole current of hiftory is to be violently oppofed, the Ireland of the Romans is to be interpreted into the prefent Scotland, and the Scotch are to be made the Aborigines of Caledonia. This conduct refults from fuch a littlenefs of foul, and betrays fuch a vulgarity of prejudice and paffion, that candour would gladly hefitate to believe, if fact did not convince her of the truth of it.

The firft appearance of this wayward folly was in the writings of Sir George Mackenzie, the firft Scotch author, I think, who dared, however gently, to reject all the ruder and earlier fictions of the national hiftory [1]. The adhering remains of the legendary fpirit of the times, it appeared coæval with the firft dawn of hiftorical liberty in Scotland, and has remained the com-

[1] In his Defence of the royal line of Scotland, 1685, in anfwer to Bp. Lloyd's Hiftorical account of Church-government, 1684, and in his Further Defence, 1686, in reply to Bp. Stillingfleet's Animadverfions prefixed to his Origines Sacræ, 1685. Sir George was affifted in thefe works by Sir Robert Sibbald, Sir James Dalrymple, and feveral other Scotch antiquarians (See Dalrymple's Collections, 1705, p. 1. Preface). And Sir George, in p. 359 &c. vol. I. of all his works, repeatedly but filently rejects all the long accounts of the Scots before Fergus I, and fo boldly cuts off a whole millennium from their hiftory.

panion

panion and the dishonour of it to the present period [1]. And the same spirit has been particularly cultivated, within these few years, by two gentlemen of real learning and considerable talents. One of them, James Macpherson Esq;, to whom the friends of poetry and history must acknowledge themselves greatly indebted, for calling out the Poems of Ossian from their original obscurity in an unknown language and an unvisited corner of the island, and for giving them to us in a version that seems to be at once bold and faithful, all animation, harmony, and grace; this gentleman, in his prefaces and notes to those poems, revived and enlarged the system of Sir George, pursued and invigorated his attempts, and violently engaged the Caledonian bard in the contest. Mr. Macpherson was seconded in the year 1768 by John Macpherson D. D. a minister in the Isle of Sky, and the author of Critical Dissertations on the Origin &c. of the ancient Caledonians, the Picts, and the Scots. This work, the intended

---

[1] In Sir Robert Sibbald's treatise on the Thule of the ancients, published in Wallace's Orkney Islands, 1693, and in Gibson's Camden, 1695; in Sir James Dalrymple's Collections for the Scottish history, 1705; in Dr. Mackenzie's Preface to his Lives of Scots writers, vol. III. fol. 1708; in Dr. Abercromby's Martial Atchievements of the Scots nation, in vol. II. fol. 1711; and in a Mr. Malcolm's Caledonian Letters, about 1738, I think.

6 THE GENUINE HISTORY OF

publication of which was repeatedly announced to the world, fome years before its appearance, in a ſtrain of high commendation by Mr. Macpherfon¹, feems to have been alfo refcued by him from the fate often incident to pofthumous productions, and was, I fuppofe, actually prefaced by him. And, in thefe agreeable and fenfible differtations, an intimate acquaintance with the Highland language, and no inconfiderable knowledge of ancient hiftory, have been made the inftruments to wreft the hiftorical accounts of the ancients from their true bafis, and to pufh afide the whole fyftem of the Caledonian and Irifh Hiftory from its fixed and natural center. And Mr. Macpherfon has lately clofed the attack in a regular and formal difquifition upon the fame principles. With a knowledge of the

---

¹ In the preface to vol. I. of Offian it is faid: " It was at " firſt intended to prefix to Offian's Poems a difcourfe con- " cerning the ancient inhabitants of Britain ; but as a Gen- " tleman in the North of Scotland, who has thoroughly ex- " amined the antiquities of this ifland, and is perfectly ac- " quainted with all the branches of the Celtic tongue, is juſt " now preparing for the prefs a work on that fubject, the " curious are referred to it." And in the Differtation prefixed to vol. II. are thefe words: " This fubject I have only lightly " touched upon, as it is to be difcuffed with more perfpicuity, " and at a much greater length, by a Gentleman, who has " thoroughly examined the antiquities of Britain and Ireland." p. xix.

Highland

Highland language superior to the Doctor's, and with a much deeper insight into ancient history, he has brought the whole collected weight of evidence together, and has concentrated all the scattered rays of the argument into a single point. With a faculty of thinking uncommonly vigorous and lively, and with a flow of language peculiarly elegant and spirited, he has given such additional strength to the argument, and has thrown such an attractive gloss over his reasonings, that to mere modern innovations he lends all the semblance of antiquity, he persuades us where he does not convince, and bribes us over to his party with all history and reason against him.

In the only volume of the History of Manchester which has yet been published, some desire had been shewed, and some pains had been taken, to clear up the original annals of Caledonia and Ireland, and to rescue both from the folly of ancient fictions on the one hand, and from the wildness of modern perversions on the other. But Mr. Macpherson's Introduction, which was published about three weeks after it, has thrown us back in the progress of historical knowledge, and has once more involved the annals in all the sophistry of fiction and fancy. This therefore is a peculiar call upon me, to vindicate the notices thus indirectly attacked by Mr. Macpherson, and,

and, what is of much more confequence in itfelf, to affert the violated principles of hiftorical faith, to protect the infulted caufe of ancient hiftory, and to eftablifh the annals of Caledonia and Ireland upon their former bafis. And I willingly obey the call. With all the deference that is due to Mr. Macpherfon as a gentleman of genius and fentiment, I fhall regularly purfue his accounts and his reafonings, as they fucceffively prefent themfelves in his pages. Difdaining the little artifices of controverfy, too honourable, I hope, to create the faults that I cannot find, and too candid, I truft, to urge ftrongly the mere failings of humanity; I fhall not expatiate upon little inaccuracies of expreffion, and I fhall not triumph over little miftakes in facts. I fhall confine myfelf to the tranfactions of the Britons before and after their fettlement in this ifland. And I fhall not merely refer to the pages in Mr. Macpherfon for the paffages that I mean to combat. This mode of proceeding, not being fufficiently diftinct and accurate with regard to the erroneous words and obnoxious affertions, is frequently the caufe of various miftakes in the writer, and is almoft fure to leave the reader in a maze of uncertainty and doubt. Not to counteract my own purpofes, I fhall conftantly produce Mr. Macpherfon's arguments in his own words.

words. Not to injure Mr. Macpherson's reasonings by maiming them, I shall give them in the quotation all the extent and force that they have in the original. And I shall place my reply at the foot, and point it directly at the heart, of each.

CHAP.

CHAP. I.

CONCERNING THE FIRST COLONY THAT MR. MACPHERSON BRINGS INTO BRITAIN.

PAG. 7, 8. The Phocæans founding Marfeilles " when the elder Tarquin is faid to
" have held the reins of government at Rome,
" the improvements introduced by the Pho-
" cæans had a great and fudden effect upon the
" manners of the Gauls. Agriculture, before
" imperfectly underftood, was profecuted with
" vigour and fuccefs. The means of fubfiftence
" being augmented, population increafed of
" courfe; migrating expeditions were formed,
" to eafe the country of its number of inhabi-
" tants.—Spain, Italy,—were filled with colonies
" from Gaul."

Here the vigorous profecution of agriculture, and the augmented means of fubfiftence, are confidered as the original caufe of emigrations. But furely this is afferted in oppofition equally to

found

found reasoning and universal experience. The increase in the population of any kingdom, so far as it is occasioned merely by the increase in the means of subsistence, will only be in an adequate proportion to it. The immediate cause, and the immediate effect, will be exactly equivalent. And consequently the improvements in agriculture can never be productive of migrations. This is obvious reasoning, embarrassed by no intricacies and obscured by no refinements of thought. And the uninterrupted experience of the world confirms the truth of it. The wretched provision that is furnished to the common people of Ireland and the Highlands, is continually impelling them into other countries. And the infinite multiplication of the necessaries and comforts of life in England, is as continually drawing the lower ranks of both into Southern Britain.—But I proceed to the history.

The original incident in this long chain of events, the settlement of the Phocæans in Gaul, is fixed to the reign of the elder Tarquin. The communication of their improved agriculture to the neighbouring Gauls, the general adoption of it by all the various and military tribes of that extensive country, the augmentation in the means of subsistence, the increase in the state of population, and this rising at last to such an extreme degree, that they, who before only " wandered " after their cattle or game over the face" of the
country,

country[1], were obliged to difburden themfelves by detaching large colonies into the neighbouring regions; all thefe fucceffive events, even in the moft fudden and rapid confecution of incidents, muft neceffarily have taken up one or two ages. And yet the migration into Italy particularly is fixed, by the very authority that Mr. Macpherfon quotes for it, in the very reign during which the Phocæans are faid immediately before to have fettled in Gaul. De tranfitu in Italiam Gallorum hæc accepimus, fays Livy in Mr. Macpherfon's own note: Prifco Tarquinio Romæ regnante,—Ambigatus,—exonerare prægravente turbâ regnum cupiens, Bellovefum ac Sigovefum—miffurum fe effe in quas Dii dediffent auguriis fedes oftendit. Bellovefo in Italiam viam Dii dederunt. And Mr. Macpherfon thus explicitly afferts the fame in p. 9, " The Gauls — " firft entered Italy, according to Livy, in the " reign of the elder Tarquin." Thefe migrations therefore were actually coæval with the fettlement at Marfeilles, and could not be occafioned by any remote confequences refulting from it. And the expedition into Italy, particularly, was actually undertaken *before* the fettlement of the Phocæans in Gaul. It was begun, and Bellovefus had already advanced to the foot of the Alps, when the news arrived of the Phocæan de-

[1] P. 7.

fcent

scent at Marseilles. And this appears even from the account to which Mr. Macpherson has referred us for the contrary. Bellovesus—, profectus ingentibus peditum equitumque copiis, in Tricastinos venit. Alpes inde oppositæ erant—.Ibi quum velut septos montium altitudo teneret Gallos, circumspectarentque quanam per juncta cœlo juga in alium orbem terrarum transirent,—allatum est, advenas quærentes agrum ab Salyum gente oppugnari. Massilienses erant hi, navibus a Phocæa profecti [1]. And Mr. Macpherson's first principle is entirely overborne by the weight of his own authorities, and by the force of his own acknowledgements.

And another objection of the same nature seems to lie as strongly against it. Mr. Macpherson seems to have written this part of his dissertation with all the hasty vivacity of a man of genius, pursuing a train of new and splendid ideas, but not rigidly examining their uniformity and agreement with each other.—The same civilized Grecians, that are said to have settled in Gaul, and to have thereby introduced a more improved agriculture into it, are equally said to have previously settled in Italy. " The Pe-
" lasgi of Peloponnesus and the islands of
" the Archipelago were the first of the Euro-
" pean Nomades who quitted the ambulatory
" life of their ancestors and applied themselves

[1] Livy, l. v. c. 34.

" to

" to the arts of civil life.—Improving their navi-
" gation by degrees, they failed to the weft,
" feized upon the neareft coaft of Italy, and
" moving into the heart of that country, met
" with the Umbri, and rofe into a mixed nation
" under the name of Latins. Extending their na-
" vigation ftill further,—the Phocæans made an
" eftablifhment on the coaft of Gaul [1]." The
earlier Pelafgi therefore muft have introduced
the arts of civil life into Italy, as the later did
into Gaul. And an improved agriculture muft
have been brought into Italy fome time before
it was carried into Gaul. The earlier Pelafgi
alfo, actually fettling in the heart of Italy, and
actually mixing with the natives in it, muft have
had a much greater communication with the Ita-
lians than the Phocæans could have had with
the Gauls, and muft have propagated all the
arts of their country with much greater fuccefs.
And the confequences deduced by Mr. Macpherfon from the introduction of the Grecian agriculture into Gaul, muft have been equally and
more early the confequences of it in Italy ; and
the migrations occafioned by it muft therefore
have been, not incurfions from Gaul into Italy,
but expeditions from Italy into Gaul. This muft
obvioufly have been the cafe, according to
Mr. Macpherfon's own reprefentations and reafonings. And the foundation of his fyftem

[1] P. 7.

is here a second time destroyed by the very hand that is employed in laying it.

P. 6—9. " The Scythians of the western Europe were, for the first time, mentioned under the name of Celtæ, by Herodotus, in the Eighty-seventh Olympiad. To investigate the origin of that appellation, we must return into a period of remote antiquity. The Pelasgi of Peloponnesus—sailed to the west, seized upon the nearest coast of Italy, and —made an establishment on the coast of Gaul—. The improvements introduced by them had a great and sudden effect upon the manners of the Gauls. Agriculture—was prosecuted—. Population increased—; migrating expeditions were formed to ease the country of its number of inhabitants, and the regions of Europe — received succeffive swarms of Gallic emigrants. — This revolution in the north of Europe extended to the greater part of its inhabitants the appellation of Celtæ, which is an adjective derived from Gael, the aboriginal name of the inhabitants of antient Gaul."

The original and primary cause of the Gallic emigrations, is here plainly afferted to be the improved agriculture communicated to them by the Grecians. This had a " great and sudden " effect

" effect upon the manners of the Gauls," producing migrations. And therefore the Gauls, according to this reprefentation, had never formed any migrating expeditions before. But in p. 9, immediately after the words above, we are told, that " though the expeditions of the " Gauls, fubfequent to the fettlement of the " Phocæans in their country, are the firft men- " tioned in hiftory, we have reafon to believe " that they pervaded Europe with their migrating " armies in a more remote period of antiquity." And furely thefe two reprefentations will not mingle and unite together. The introduction of an improved agriculture by the Grecians either was or was not, in Mr. Macpherfon's opinion, the original and remotely efficient caufe of the Gallic migrations. If it was, Mr. Macpherfon can have no reafon to believe, that the Gauls pervaded Europe with their migrating armies in a remoter period of Antiquity. And if it was not, the great and fudden effect, which it is here defcribed to have had upon the manners of the Gauls, is all a delufion and vifion.

This hiftory of the Pelafgian refinements imported into Gaul, and producing migrations from it, is given us in order to account for the name of Celtæ being affixed to the general body of the Weft-Europeans. And the migrations occafioned by the improved ftate of agriculture, are faid to have carried the colonies and the

name of the Gael or Celtæ over many of the regions of Europe. Yet "we have reason to
" believe," as we are told in p. 9, " that the
" Gauls pervaded Europe with their migrating
" armies in a more remote period of antiquity."
And therefore, according to Mr. Macpherson himself, they must equally, in a more remote period, have planted the colonies and the name of the Celtæ in many of the regions of Europe.

Thus does this ingenious writer go on, apparently counteracting his own purposes and refuting his own positions. And I wrest nothing. I wish to give every passage its full import. And I desire to put an end to the examination, when I cease to prosecute it with candour.

P. 9. " The appellation of Celtæ — is an
" adjective derived from Gael, the aboriginal
" name of the inhabitants of ancient Gaul."

I feel a little reluctance in myself to enter the field of Celtic etymology with Mr. Macpherson. A gentleman, who was bred, I apprehend, in the bosom of the Highlands, an author, who, as the translator of Ossian, must certainly be conversant with the best and oldest writers in the Erse, should naturally command such a clear and extensive view of the language, its principles, and its genius, as to deter any mere Englishman
from

from the unequal conteſt. But, to be deterred by ſuch reaſons, is to betray an ignorance in the workings of the human heart. A conſciouſneſs of ſuperior knowledge, in any department of literature, almoſt always ſeduces a writer into a careleſſneſs and injudiciouſneſs in the exertion of it.

In the Hiſtory of Mancheſter I have endeavoured to inveſtigate the origin of the name of Celtæ. I have there proved it, I think, not to be an adjective derived from Gael, but to be equally a ſubſtantive, and actually the ſame word, with it. And, as it is neceſſary for the ſolution of the preſent difficulty, and will be ſerviceable for the diſcuſſion of ſome future doubts, I ſhall here go over the argument again, and contract it into a ſmaller compaſs.—The Iriſh and the Highlanders reciprocally denominate themſelves by the general title of Cael, Gael, or Gauls. They alſo diſtinguiſh themſelves, as the Welſh originally did, and as the Welſh diſtinguiſh them both at preſent, by the appellation of Guidhil, Guæthel, and Gathel. And this is certainly the origin of the other. The intermediate TH being left quieſcent in the pronunciation, as it is in many words of the Britiſh language, Gathel would immediately be formed into Gael. And Gathel is actually ſounded like Gael by both the Iriſh and the Highlanders at preſent. The appellation of Gathel therefore was originally the same with Gael, and the parent of it. But this is not all. The quiescent letters in British are frequently transferred from the middle to the conclusion of the word, where they are no longer quiescent; and as Needle is popularly changed into Neeld in Lancashire, and Kathair is formed into Carth and Garth, so Gathel is changed into Galath, Galat, Galt, and Celt. And we see the fact directly exemplified in the Gael of the Continent being universally denominated Galatæ and Celtæ by the Grecians, and Gallt and Gallta by the Irish. The appellations therefore of Gathel-i, Gall-i, Galat-æ, Calet-es, An-Calit-es, and Celt-æ, are all one and the same denomination, only varied by the astonishing ductility of the Celtic, and only disguised by the alterations ever incident to a language that has been merely oral for ages [1].

P. 8, 9. In consequence of the Phocæan settlement at Marseilles, "Spain, Italy,—and the British
" Isles were filled with colonies from Gaul, in
" whom the old inhabitants, if they differed ori-
" ginally from the Gael, were lost."

And in p. 26, where the same subject is retouched, Mr. Macpherson speaks thus.—" The

[1] See History of Manchester, p. 437—439.

" Umbri

" Umbri, who were the most ancient inhabi-
" tants of Italy (Umbrorum gens antiquissima
" Italiæ existimatur. Plin. lib. iii. Umbri anti-
" quissimus Italiæ populus. Flor. lib. i.), were
" the posterity of Gauls who penetrated into
" that country long before the commencement
" of history (Bocchus absolvit Gallorum veterum
" propaginem Umbros esse. Solin. lib. viii. Umbri
" prima veterum Gallorum proles. August. in
" Sempron. Umbros veterum Gallorum esse pro-
" paginem Marcus Antonius refert. Servius in
" Æneid. xii.). We may naturally suppose that
" the Gauls of Belgium would have found less dif-
" ficulty in crossing a very narrow channel into
" Britain than their countrymen at the foot of
" the Alps in clambering, with their wives and
" children, over the vast ridge of mountains
" which separated them from Italy. It may
" therefore be concluded, that Britain received
" very considerable colonies from the Belgic di-
" vision of Gaul as early, at least, as the Gael of
" the Alpin regions seized upon Italy under the
" name of Umbri."

In these passages are contained two assertions concerning the first population of Britain, one urged as probably true, and the other produced as certainly so. According to the former, the natives of Gaul settled in Italy, under the name of Umbri, long before the commencement of history, and may therefore be concluded to have transported

ported themselves as early into Britain. And the latter declares the British Isles to have received a colony of the Celtæ, in confequence of the Phocæan fettlement at Marfeilles. I fhall confider both of thefe attentively.

The opinion here advanced by Mr. Macpherfon, concerning the Umbri, has been advanced by feveral writers before, in that ftrange humour which has been taken up by fo many antiquarians, of magnifying the glory and extending the pofleflions of the Celtæ. But the notion appears to be chimerical and groundlefs.

The Umbri are affirmed by both Pliny and Florus, as Mr. Macpherfon himfelf has quoted them, to be the moft antient people in Italy, or, in other words, to be the progeny of the firft colonifts that came into it after the flood. And if the Umbri were a race of men derived from Gaul, Gaul muft have been inhabited fome ages before Italy. So acceflible as the latter is acrofs the fea from Dalmatia or from Germany by land, and therefore lying much more obvious than Gaul to the great colonies of the Noachidæ, as they converged to the Weft; it muft, according to this reprefentation, have never received any colony at all, till Gaul difcharged its fuperfluous numbers into it. A country that muft have peculiarly invited the fpreading hords of the Eaft, as pufhing its whole length in one vaft projection into the waves of the Mediterranean, and therefore lore lying very happily central betwixt the three great divisions of the globe, is here supposed to have continued totally wild and desolate, even for ages after Gaul was inhabited, till the Celtæ had gradually spread themselves 'over all Gaul, till they began to increase in numbers, till they were obliged to diffuse themselves into other countries, and till they were compelled even " to clamber, with their wives and children, over " the vast ridge of mountains which separated " them from Italy." This is such an account, as confronts every suggestion of reason, and outrages every principle of propriety. The bands, that filed through the forests of Germany into Gaul, must equally have found their way through the vallies of the Tyrolese into Italy. The tribes, that coasted from Greece or Dalmatia into Gaul, must previously have landed upon the shore of Italy. As the great tide of European population rolled directly from the plains of Shinar to the verge of the Atlantic, in the natural course of causes and effects, no country could have been primarily inhabited from the West. And Italy peculiarly could not, open as it is on the East and its collateral points, having its northern mountains remarkably pierced with a valley through the whole breadth of them, and being compleatly closed up and barricaded by its natural ramparts on the North-West, the only point in which it borders upon Gaul. As

the

the natives of Gaul therefore can never be admitted to have been the first planters of Italy, the Umbri can never be allowed to have been originally a colony from Gaul. And Mr. Macpherson must either deny the Umbri to have been the most antient people of Italy, or admit them not to have been originally derived from Gaul.

This reasoning is sufficient to counterbalance the assertions of such authors, as Mr. Macpherson has produced in support of the opinion. And the reasoning is happily confirmed by an historian of the most respectable character, and with whom, in a comparative estimate of authenticity and knowledge, Mr. Macpherson's writers are but mere flutterers in the regions of history. Livy asserts the first and earliest migration of the Gauls to have been only in the reign of the elder Tarquin, and about 600 years before Christ. And he is uncommonly accurate and circumstantial in his account. Gallos—eos qui oppugnaverunt Clusium non fuisse qui primi Alpes transierint, satis constat. Ducentis quippe annis antequam Clusium oppugnarent urbemque Romam caperent, in Italiam Galli transcenderunt.— De transitu in Italiam Gallorum hæc accepimus. Prisco Tarquinio Romæ regnante,—Bellovefo— in Italiam viam Dii dederunt.—Profectus ingentibus peditum equitumque copiis, in Tricastinos venit. Alpes inde oppositæ erant, quas inexsuperabiles visas haud equidem miror, nullâ dum'

via

viâ (quod quidem continens memoria fit, nifi de Hercule fabulis credere libet) fuperatas. Crofſing the Alps, fufifque acie Tufcis, haud procul Ticino flumine—condidere urbem, Mediolanum appellarunt. Alia fubinde manus, — Elitovio duce, — favente Bellovefo, quum tranfcendiſſet Alpes, ubi nunc Brixia ac Verona urbes funt— confidunt. Poſt hos Salluvii — circa Ticinum amnem —. Deinde Boii Lingones —, quum jam inter Padum atque Alpes omnia tenerentur, Pado ratibus trajecto, non Etrufcos modò, fed etiam Umbros, agro pellunt. Tum Senones, recentiſſimi advenarum, attacked Clufium and burnt Rome [1]. And the regular detail of fuch an hiſtorian fixes the point beyond all poſſibility of doubt. The Gauls firſt entered Italy about the year 600 before Chriſt, when the country was compleatly inhabited from end to end.

But the authors quoted by Mr. Macpherfon have been wronged in the application by him. The Umbri might be the defcendants of antient Gauls, and even the firſt inhabitants of Italy; and yet not be derivatives from Gaul. As the great body of the Celtæ puſhed by land or coaſted by fea for the feat of their future Empire in Gaul, a part of them might divide from the reſt, and make a fettlement in Italy. And this appears, I think, to have been actually the cafe. That the Umbri were really Celtæ or Gauls, is

[1] L. v. c. 33.—35.

aſſerted

asserted by such authorities, as, however insignificant in themselves, we cannot in justice reject without a superior authority to the contrary. And the remains of Celtic or Gallic appellations among the Umbri, is a strong confirmation of their assertions. I shall mention only two, because they must both have been prior to any migration of colonies from Gaul. And these are their own national and original appellation of Umbri, and the similar appellation of their originally principal river, the Umbrio, both evidently the same with the Umbri and the Humber in Britain; the generical appellation of the Celtæ in Italy and in this island being communicated by both to a great æstuary or river in their country, and our Humber being therefore written and pronounced Chumber formerly [1].

A migration then from Gaul into Italy, before the reign of Tarquin the First, is precluded by the positive voice of history. And all inferences derived from the supposition must equally fall with it to the ground. A migration from Gaul into Britain, as early at least as the other, is inferred from it by Mr. Macpherson. And the conclusion is reasonable in itself. But the premises have been here proved to be false. And Mr. Macpherson must refer his first colony from Gaul to the æra of the Phocæan establishment in it.

[1] Carte, vol. i. p. 17.

The former opinion was given to us only as probable. This is prefented as certain. And it challenges for its fupport the authority of Cæfar and the teftimony of Tacitus. Tacitus is quoted thus, In univerfum tamen æftimanti Gallos vicinum folum occupaffe, credibile eft; and Cæfar thus, Britanni non multum a Gallicâ differunt confuetudine. But one of thefe authorities is not quoted fairly. The latter, which is here applied to the Britons in oppofition to the Belgæ [1], and has the word Britanni added to it in order to make it applicable, actually relates to the Belgæ in oppofition to the Britons, is actually referred to the Belgæ by Mr. Macpherfon himfelf in p. 33, and actually relates only to the Belgæ of Kent. And even if both thefe paffages were fairly quoted, they very obvioufly determine neither the fact nor the period of the Gallic fettlement in Gaul. They prove indeed the very high probability of a Gallic colony originally fettling in the ifland: but they evince not the certainty of it. And they do not give us the leaft intimation concerning the particular æra of the fettlement. Mr. Macpherfon, deriving the fettlement in a long confecution of caufes and effects from the Phocæan eftablifhment in Gaul, fixes the æra one or two centuries after the eftablifhment, and about 400 or 500 years before Chrift. But Mr. Macpherfon alfo fixes the æra

[1] See 2d and 3d Sections of this chapter.

exactly

exactly at the period of that establishment, as he ranks the migration into Britain coæval with the expedition into Italy. Tacitus and Cæsar, however, lend not the smallest sanction to either part of Mr. Macpherson's chronology. And, even if Mr. Macpherson's authority could be of any moment on a subject of this nature, its own contradictoriness must destroy itself.

This is the whole of Mr. Macpherson's argument with respect to the coming of the first colonists into Britain. And I am sorry to observe on reviewing the whole, that, in the progress of the argument, Mr. Macpherson seems to be unhappy in every movement. And the period and the fact of a Gallic colony originally settling in Britain, which are the first great points in Mr. Macpherson's historical system, are left absolutely doubtful and undetermined.—But as these are two particulars of some consequence in the history of Britain, the great design of the present work, to enlighten the dark period of its earlier annals, naturally leads me to endeavour to ascertain them. It must be hazardous indeed to attempt, where Mr. Macpherson has failed. But it can be no disgrace to be baffled, where even he has been unsuccessful.

The derivation of the Britons from the Gauls does not depend, as Tacitus and Cæsar have placed it, upon any precarious reasonings from the vicinity of the two countries and a similarity in the two nations. It may be grounded upon better principles. And it is clearly demonstrated by the national appellation of Gaul, which I have already shewn in part, and shall fully shew hereafter, to have been formerly, or to be at present, retained by the British inhabitants in every quarter of the island. This proof is equally short and decisive. But the period, in which the Gauls first crossed the channel into Britain, is much more difficult to be ascertained. It may, I think, be settled in this manner.

The first migration of the Gauls that is recorded by history, as I have already shewn, was made in the reign of the elder Tarquin and about the year 600 before Christ. This was a double one, an expedition into Italy, and an invasion of Germany [1]. And this was clearly after Britain had been peopled by the Gauls. As long as the Gauls had a vent for their growing numbers into the uninhabited regions of Spain or of Britain, they could not have been obliged to turn back upon their progenitors behind them. The great current of European population, which had fallen for ages into the West, could not have been compelled to return upon itself, till it had

[1] Livy, l. v. c. 33.

filled

filled the whole extent of its intended channel, and till it found itself stopt in its progress by insuperable barriers. And the Gauls would certainly not have chosen to enter Italy and invade Germany, where they were sure to encounter opposition, and where their settlements must be precarious from the uncertainty of their success, and exposed to danger from the remoteness of their countrymen; when all the region of Britain, in particular, lay open to them, was ready to receive their colonies, and by its daily appearance to the eye seemed actually to invite them into it. At this period, therefore, the island of Britain was certainly inhabited. And it must have been inhabited long before.

When the Gauls first began to discharge their numbers into Britain, the island would naturally serve as the great reservoir of the continent for ages. Gradually as the people multiplied to be troublesome, they would all find a safe and easy conveyance into Britain. And Gaul could not begin to be overburdened with her progeny, till the population of Britain was nearly compleated, till the uninhabited parts of the island were too remote from the continent, or till the islanders were obliged, in their own defence, to forbid any future migrations into the country. This must have been the actual state of population in Britain, for some time before the expeditions of Bellovesus and Sigovesus from Gaul. And fresh colo-

colonies, for some time before, must have ceased to find their way into Britain. The tribes of Gaul were now pent up within their own continent. And as the multiplication continued, and all the former resources were exhausted, they were obliged at last to recoil upon the more easterly colonies, to explore an unpractised way over the snows and mountains of the Alps, and to open to themselves a new receptacle among the inhabitants of Italy and Germany. A long time therefore must have elapsed, before the superfluous numbers of Gaul could have filled up the greater part of the island, and could have any occasion to prohibit the entrance of any more into it. And some time must have intervened, before the effect of this prohibition could have appeared upon the continent, and more, before it could have burst out in the great and necessary migrations into Germany and Italy. Four or five centuries must have passed betwixt the commencement of population in the island, and the æra of those migrations on the continent. And the position is strikingly confirmed to us by the parallel history of Ireland, this island in a later period serving equally as a drain to Britain, and the population of it not being compleated in less than 500 years [1].

This reasoning settles the first inhabitation of Britain about 1000 years before Christ. About

[1] See History of Manchester, p. 433—437. and 440—442.

1000 years before Chrift it is actually fixed by fome of Richard's authorities: A. M. 3000, circa hæc tempora cultam & habitatam primùm Britanniam arbitrantur nonnulli [1]. And about 1000 years before Chrift the progrefs of population, as far as it can be traced in the ifland, concurs with the argument to fettle it [2]. From the one reafon it may be concluded, that the ifland was firft inhabited no lefs than this number of years before the Chriftian æra. And from the other it appears highly probable, that the ifland could not have been inhabited many more before it. And the coincidence of two fuch arguments, that derived from the ftate of population on the continent, and this deduced from the progrefs of population in the ifland, the concurrence of both with the authorities of hiftory, and the convergence of all to one common point of time, give us as much certainty on the fubject, as we muft ever expect in enquiries of this very remote nature, and fix the firft migration of the Gauls into Britain, with as much precifion as the difficulties of the queftion will admit, about a thoufand years before the coming of our Saviour, or about the reigns of David and Solomon among the Jews.

[1] P. 50.   [2] Hift. of Manch. p. 7. and 466.

II.

II.

CONCERNING THE SECOND COLONY THAT MR. MACPHERSON BRINGS INTO BRITAIN.

PAG. 10. " The domestic improvements
" which, in the beginning of their progress
" in Gaul, enabled the inhabitants of that coun-
" try to overrun the regions of the West and
" North, had arrived at some degree of maturity
" long before the Romans penetrated beyond
" the Alps. Instead of wandering in search of
" foreign settlements, the Gauls found it more
" convenient to cultivate those which they al-
" ready possessed. The spirit of conquest re-
" tired further towards the North; and the
" tide of migration, which had for ages flowed
" from Gaul, returned upon itself —. The Ger-
" man Celtæ repassed the Rhine."

The improvements in agriculture are here, and in p. 8, said to have consequentially occasioned the migrations of the Gauls. But here they are equally said to have put an end to them. And the same natural cause has two different and contra-

D   dictory

dictory effects attributed to it.—The improvements in agriculture are declared to have occasioned migrations in the beginning of their progress, and in their advancement towards maturity to have given an absolute termination to them. And the same natural cause, that in its weaker and commencing operations produced one effect, in its stronger and more perfect influence produced another and the opposite.—All this, I think, is clearly asserted together in the present extract. " The domestic improvements —, in the " beginning of their progress in Gaul, enabled " the inhabitants — to overrun the regions of " the West and North —." When they " had " arrived at some degree of maturity —, instead " of wandering in search of foreign settlements, " the Gauls found it more convenient to culti- " vate those which they already possessed."— Nor is this all the inconsistency which this extract seems to contain. Those improvements, which in their infant state impelled the Gauls to relinquish their country, in their maturer condition not only induced them to stay at home, but even brought foreign emigrants into the country. " The tide of migration, which had " for ages flowed from Gaul, returned upon it- " self."

That multiplied population, which was the immediate consequence of the commencing improvements in agriculture, obliged the Gauls to discharge

charge themselves in colonies into the neighbouring countries. That infinitely greater population, which must have equally resulted from the improvements being more generally diffused, more experimentally known, and considerably heightened in their influence, and which must have obliged the Gauls, in an infinitely greater degree, to discharge themselves into the neighbouring regions; this, it seems, did not oblige them at all, this actually prevailed upon them to stay at home, and this absolutely invited others into the country. Thus does this lively and valuable writer again seem to be engaged at cross purposes with his own argument.

P. 11, 12. " More than three centuries prior " to the Christian æra, the German Celtæ, " under the name of Cimbri, ravaged all the " regions lying between the Rhine and the Ionian " sea (Hæ sunt nationes quæ tam longè ab suis " sedibus Delphos profectæ sunt. Cicero pro " Fonteio, xx.)."

The passage, here cited by Mr. Macpherson, actually stands in a striking opposition to his doctrine. It refers not to the Cimbri, or German Celtæ, at all. It refers solely and absolutely to the Proper Celtæ, or the natives of Gaul. —Cicero, vindicating the conduct of Fronteius in his

his government of Gaul, Provinciæ Galliæ M. Fronteius præfuit, and, like a mere advocate, catching at the popular prejudices of the Romans, says thus of the Gallic tribes. Hæ funt nationes quæ tam longè ab fuis fedibus Delphos ufque, ad Apollinem Pythium atque ad oraculum orbis terræ vexandum ac fpoliandum, profectæ funt. *Ab iifdem gentibus — obfeffum eft Capitolium.* Here we fee no mention of the Cimbri, and no intimation concerning the German Celtæ. All that is faid is fpoken merely of the real and abfolute Gauls, of thofe who facked Rome as well as plundered Delphi. And Mr. Macpherfon's quotation, not only does not prove the fpirit of conqueft to have retired from Gaul towards the North, and the German Celtæ to have ravaged all the regions lying between the Rhine and the Ionian Sea; but actually evinces the contrary, fhews the fpirit at this period to have been ftill very active in Gaul, and appropriates thefe ravages to the Native Celtæ.

P. 28, 29. " The fpirit of conqueft paffing
" from the Gauls to the Celto-Germanic colonies
" beyond the Rhine, the latter pervaded Europe
" with their armies (Cimbri magnam Europæ nec
" exiguam Afiæ partem fibi tributariam fecere
" agrofque debellatorum a fe occuparunt. Diod.
" Sic. lib. v.). — The German pofterity of the
" Gauls,

" Gauls, under the name of Cimbri, traverfed
" the vaft regions between their own country
" and the fea of Ionia (Cimbri contractis undique
" copiis, ad Ionicum mare converfi, gentem Illy-
" riorum, et quicquid gentium ad Macedonas
" ufque habitat, imo ipfos Macedonas opprefsere.
" Pauf. Attic. iv.). About half a century after
" the death of Alexander, they poured irrefifti-
" ble armies into Greece, Thrace, and Mace-
" donia — (Gens afpera, audax, bellicofa, domi-
" tis Pannoniis, et hortante deinde fucceffu, divi-
" fis agminibus, alii Græciam, alii Macedoniam,
" omnia ferro proterentes, petivere. Juftin. lib.
" xxiv.). — Some of them, paffing the Propon-
" tis, filled the leffer Afia with their colonies
" (Tantæ fœcunditatis juventus, ut Afiam omnem
" velut examine aliquo implerent. Juftin,
" lib. xxv.); and fpread the terror of their name
" far and wide by the invincible fortune of
" their arms (Tantus terror nominis et armorum
" invicta felicitas. Juftin, lib. xxv.). The irrup-
" tion of the Cimbri was not merely depredatory.
" They left colonies in their conquered countries
" (Agros debellatorum a fe occuparunt. Diod.
" Sic. lib. v.)."

I have cited this paffage immediately after the former, that Mr. Macpherfon's argument may enjoy the full force of the authorities produced in its favour. And, in both thefe extracts, by the fame

38 THE GENUINE HISTORY OF

over-ruling influence the Germans are regularly substituted for the Gauls. They were the natives of Gaul, and not the residents of Germany, who more than 300 years prior to the Christian æra, as the preceding passage fixes the time, or about half a century after the death of Alexander, as the present more accurately, though contradictorily, fixes it, ravaged all the country to the sea of Ionia. In the year 279 before Christ, the Gauls sent out three armies, which ravaged Pannonia, Greece, Macedonia, and Asia, plundered, or attempted to plunder, the temple at Delphi, and settled colonies in some of those countries. And even the authorities, here cited to confine these actions to the Germans, all concur to appropriate them to the Gauls. This must seem very strange. But it is actually true.

Diodorus, speaking expresly of the Gauls, but considering them as extended εξης μεχρι της Σκυθιας, says thus. *Hi — sunt qui Romam ceperunt. Hi templum in Delphis expilarunt. Hi magnam Europæ partem*, &c. Ουτοι εισιν οι την μεν Ρωμην ελοντες, το δε ιερον το εν Δελφοις συλησαντες, και πολλην μεν της Ευρωπης, ουκ ολιγην δε και της Ασιας, φορολογησαντες· οι δια την προς τες Ελληνας επιπλοκην ΕΛΛΗΝΟ-ΓΑΛΑΤΑΙ κληθεντες. Those therefore who reduced a considerable part of Europe, and no inconsiderable portion of Asia, and settled on the
lands

THE BRITONS ASSERTED. 39

lands of the conquered, were not Cimbri, though Mr. Macpherfon has unwarily interpolated the name in his quotation; were not Germans, as Mr. Macpherfon has arbitrarily interpreted his own inferted name of Cimbri to mean; but were Gauls, the fame that took Rome, the fame that plundered Delphi, and the fame that were denominated Gallo-Græci.

Paufanias in his Attica fays thus. *Galli* — in extremis Europæ oris ad vaftum mare accolunt. — Verùm ut *Galli* appellarentur, non nifi ferò ufus obtinuit. *Celtas* enim, quum ipfi fe antiquitus, tum alii eos, nominarunt. *Hi* contractis undecunque copiis, ad Ionicum mare verfi, &c. Οἱ δὲ ΓΑΛΑΤΑΙ — νεμονῖαι τῆς Ευρωπης τα εσχαῖα επι θαλασση πολλη —· οψε δε ποῖε αυῖες καλεισθαι ΓΑΛΑΤΑΣ εξενικησε· ΚΕΛΤΟΙ γαρ καῖα τε σφας το αρχαιον, και παρα τοις αλλοις, ωνομαζονῖο. Συλλεγεισα δε ΣΦΙΣΙ ςραῖια τρεπεῖαι την επι Ιονιε, ἢ το τε Ιλλυριων εθνος, και παν οσον αχρι Μακεδονων ωκει, και Μακεδονας αυῖες, αναςαῖες εποιησε. And here Mr. Macpherfon appears in his quotation to have inadvertently dropt the words Galli and Celtæ, and to have planted the word Cimbri in their place. Paufanias does not affert the German pofterity of the Gauls to have ravaged the country up to the fea of Ionia. And Paufanias does not affert any nation to have committed thefe ravages under the name of Cimbri. He declares the Gauls, and the Gauls only, to have

D 4   made

made this expedition. And he declares them to have paffed under their own indigenous denominations of Galli and Celtæ.

Juftin is the other author here quoted. And he is ftill more exprefsly againft the purpofe for which Mr. Macpherfon has produced him. He fays thus. *Galli,* abundanti multitudine, *cùm eos non caperent terræ quæ genuerant,* ad fedes novas quærendas velut ver facrum miferunt. *Ex his* portio in Italiâ confedit, *quæ et urbem Romanam captam incendit,* et portio Illyricos finus — per ftrages barbarorum penetravit, & in Pannoniâ confedit; gens afpera, audax, bellicofa —. Hortante deinde fucceffu, divifis agminibus, alii Græciam, alii Macedoniam, omnia ferro proterentes, petivere. Tantufque terror *Gallici* nominis erat, ut — folus rex Macedoniæ Ptolemæus adventum *Gallorum* intrepidus audivit. — Igitur *Galli,* duce Belgio, attacked and defeated Ptolemy. — Interea Brennus, quo duce portio *Gallorum* in Græciam fe effuderat, auditâ victoriâ fuorum qui Belgio duce Macedonas vicerant, — Delphos iter vertit [1]. And in another place Juftin fays thus. *Gallorum* eâ tempeftate tantæ fœcunditatis juventus fuit, ut Afiam omnem velut examine aliquo implerent. Denique, neque reges Orientis fine mercenario *Gallorum* exercitu ulla bella gefferunt, neque,

[1] L. xxiv. c. 4, 5, 6.

pulfi regno, ad alios quam ad *Gallos* confugerunt. Tantus terror *Gallici* nominis et armorum invicta felicitas [1]. And here Mr. Macpherson appears, in the same strain of inadvertency that is noticed before, to have left out the word Gallorum in one of his quotations, and Gallici in another, and to have applied all three in direct opposition to the express and repeated meaning of the whole. The armies which Justin here describes as pouring into Thrace, Greece, and Macedonia, he does not assert to have been Germans, and he does not affirm to have been denominated Cimbri. He explicitly declares them to have been Gauls. He directly derives them from their native country of Gaul. And he repeatedly makes them to have been a part of that national body, which took the city of Rome, and marched to plunder the temple of Delphi.

Each of these long extracts reflects a light upon the other. And from the united luster of all we may clearly see, that Mr. Macpherson has been strangely led away by his own prejudices, has pressed into his cause arguments that are all in a natural combination against him, and, in a spirit of involuntary piracy, is even fighting under false colours. The total omission of some expressions that must have disproved the application of the passages, the careful discharge of

[1] L. xxv, c. 2.

all

all hostile words from the quotations, and the officious interpolation of friendly in their room, facts that appear evident upon the face of the extracts above, certainly give an unhappy aspect of disingenuousness to the whole, and may seem to discredit the integrity and honour of Mr. Macpherson. But any one that has felt in his own breast the prevailing bias of either systematical or national prejudices, and can therefore make the proper allowance for the force of both together, will easily acquit Mr. Macpherson of any intentional frauds, and will refer all to its immediate cause, to prepossessions which have enslaved the strongest intellects, and to weaknesses which are the groundwork of all the patriot virtues.

P. 10—12. "The German Celtæ (Celtæ five Galli quos Cimbros vocant. Appian, in Illyr. —) repassed the Rhine, committed terrible devastations, and — extended their conquests to Spain —. The Lusitanians, according to Diodorus Siculus, were the most warlike branch of the Cimbri (αλκιμωτατοι μεν εισι οι καλεμενοι Λυσιτανοι. Diod. Sic. lib. v.)."

Here we meet with the same strain of false quotation, as we have already remarked in the preceding articles. — The passage in Appian, which is here applied to the German Celtæ, belongs

longs to the Native Gauls in the original. Eofdem
[Autarios] *Celtafque*, quos Cimbros vocant, *ad Delphos posuisse castra* : αὐτὰς ἐ ΚΕΛΤΟΙΣ, τοις Κιμβροις λεγομενοις, ΕΠΙ ΔΕΛΦΟΙΣ ΣΥΣΤΡΑΤΕΥΣΑΙ [1].
The Gauls, we fee, who are faid to have been denominated Cimbri, were actually Proper Celtæ, and were abfolutely the very Gauls that encamped againſt the temple of Delphi.—And the paſſage here cited from Diodorus, to prove the Luſitanians a branch of the Cimbri, is equally cited by Mr. Macpherſon only four pages before, to prove the Luſitanians a branch of the Galli, and has actually no reference to either. This is as aſtoniſhing as it is evident. Speaking of the migrations of the Galli, or Proper Celtæ, in p. 6—10, and of the much later migrations of the Cimbri, or German Celtæ, in p. 10—12, Mr. Macpherſon in p. 8 aſſerts Spain to have been filled with a colony from Gaul, as he here aſſerts it to have received another from Germany, and actually brings the fame paſſage of hiſtory as a proof of both. When he is to evince the Cimbric or Celto-Germanic ſettlement from it, as here and in p. 30, he quotes it thus, αλκιμωτατοι μεν εισι οι καλεμενοι Λυσιτανοι, and, omnium *Cimbrorum* fortiſſimi ſunt Luſitani. But when he is to prove the Gallic, he cites it thus, αλκιμωτατοι μεν ΤΩΝ ΓΑΛΑΤΩΝ οι καλεμενοι Λυσιτανοι. Mr.

[1] P. 1106. Amſtel. 1670.

Macpherson's prejudices and inadvertency throw any colour over the passage, which the nature of the present argument calls for. The same portion of history is adduced by Mr. Macpherson, and once only within four pages, to prove two absolutely opposite points. It is adduced three times; and the principal word in the original, which would have vindicated the passage from the misapplication, is studiously omitted every time. And the main essential words in the quotation are twice interpolated, and are both times different. The passage, in short, that has been thus applied to the Galli and the Cimbri, has not the least connexion with either. It refers only to the Iberes: ΤΩΝ ΔΕ ΙΒΗΡΩΝ αλκιμω]α]οι μεν εισιν οι καλεμενοι Λυσι]ανοι, says Diodorus, all along distinguishing the Iberes from the Celtæ. And, to compleat this group of inaccuracies and contradictions, this very part of Diodorus's history is referred to by Mr. Macpherson in p. 85 and 86, as containing an " exprefs testimony, " that the Iberians were a " different people " from the Celtæ.

P. 10—12. " The German Celtæ (Ιππευς δε " Γαλα]ης το γεν@·, η Κιμβρ@·. Plutarch in Ma-
" rio.) repassed the Rhine, committed terrible
" devastations, and acquired a just title to the
" name of Cimbri, which signifies a band of
"robbers

" robbers (Κιμβρας επονομαζυσι Γερμανοι τας λῃςας.
" Plutarch in Mario. λῃςρικοι ον]ες και πλανη]ες οι
" Κιμβροι. Strabo, lib. vii.)¹."

This irruption of the German Celtæ is fixed, as I have noted before, more than three centuries prior to the Chriſtian æra in p. 11; and in p. 28, about half a century after the death of Alexander, or about the year 273 before Chriſt. But, as a proof of the irruption, Mr. Macpherſon quotes the well-known paſſage of Plutarch, that relates the ſtory of a Gallic or Cimbric horſeman being ſent to murder Marius in the priſon of Minturnæ, and dropping his ſword with terror at the appearance, addreſs, and name of a man, that had made himſelf ſo formidable to his countrymen. Ιππευς—Γαλα]ης το γεν⊙, η Κιμβρ⊙, αμφο]ερως γαρ ιςορει]αι². But this paſſage evidently relates to that incurſion of the Cimbri, which happened near two centuries after either

¹ So Dr. Macpherſon interprets Cimbri, Robbers, and from the ſame incompetent authority, p. 112.

² V. II. p. 532. Bryan.—Valerius Maximus in his account of this incident ſays thus—Miſſus ad Marium occidendum in privatâ domo Minturnis clauſum ſervus publicus, natione Cimber, et ſenem et inermem et ſqualore obſitum, ſtrictum gladium tenens, aggredi non ſuſtinuit, ſed claritate viri obcæcatus, abjecto ferro, attonitus inde ac tremens fugit. Cimbrica nimirum calamitas oculos hominis perſtrinxit, devictæque ſuæ gentis interitus animum comminuit: etiam Diis immortalibus indignum ratis, ab uno ejus Nationis interfici Marium, quam totam deleverat. L. ii. c. 10. §. 6. Delphin.

period,

period, which was made acrofs the Rhine about 112, and was terminated by Marius about 101, before the Chriftian æra.

And the intimation here given, that the German Celtæ acquired the name of Cimbri after they had paffed the Rhine, and after they had committed terrible devaftations in Gaul, appeals for its authority to another paffage of Plutarch, which fays not, that the name was given on the Gallic fide of the Rhine, but on the German, which fays not, that the Gauls conferred the appellation upon them, but that the Germans ufually called a robber a Cimber. So much is the proof in oppofition to the point!

P. 28, 29. " The German pofterity of the
" Gauls, under the name of Cimbri,—cut to
" pieces all the intermediate nations between
" their original feats and the Hellefpont (Ex-
" torres inopiâ agrorum, profecti domo, per af-
" perrimam Illyrici oram, Pæoniam inde et
" Thraciam, pugnando cum ferociffimis genti-
" bus, menfi has terras ceperunt. Livius, lib.
" xxxviii.)."

I have produced this paffage again with the new quotation annexed to it, to point out another inftance of the ftrange inaccuracy which runs through the prefent work.—In p. 24 we are told

told, that " the Gael of the continent extended
" their name with their arms into all the regions
" of Europe ;" and we have this quotation to
confirm it, " Ferox natio Gallorum pervagata
" bello prope orbem terrarum. Livius, lib.
" xxxviii." The former citation is brought to
prove the irruptions of the Cimbri or German
Celtæ, in opposition to the Gael or Native Celtæ.
The latter is produced to prove the irruptions
of the Gael or Native Celtæ, in contradistinction
to the Cimbri or German Celtæ. And yet the
two passages, that are thus applied to two different nations, are actually parts of one and the
same account, and are directly spoken of one
and the same people. The whole passage runs
thus. Manlius in *Gallo-Græciâ* bellum gessit—.
Hi Galli,—seu inopiâ agri seu prædæ spe, nullam gentium, per quas ituri essent, parem rati,
Brenno duce in Dardanos pervenerunt—.Non
me præterit, Milites, says Manlius to his soldiery, omnium quæ Asiam colunt gentium *Gallos*
famâ belli præstare. Inter mitissimum genus hominum ferox natio, pervagata bello propè orbem
terrarum, sedem cepit.—Semel primo congressu
ad Alliam olim fuderunt majores nostros : ex eo
tempore per ducentos jam annos, pecorum in
modum, consternatos cædunt fugantque —. Et
illis majoribus nostris cum *haud dubiis Gallis in
terrâ suâ genitis* res erat. Hi jam degeneres sunt,
mixti, et *Gallo-Græci* verè, quod appellantur.—

Extorres

Extorres inopiâ agrorum, profecti domo, per asperrimam Illyrici oram, Pæoniam inde et Thraciam, pugnando cum ferocissimis gentibus, emensi, has terras ceperunt. But now mansuefacta est feritas [1]. What Mr. Macpherson has given in one place to the Native Gauls, and in another to the German Celtæ, relates only to the former, we see. And the inconsistency in the application is a remarkable instance of inattention in the author.

P. 10—12. " The German Celtæ (Celtæ sive " Galli quos [Cimbros vocant. Appian. in Illyr. " Ἱππευς δε Γαλάτης το γενος, η Κιμβρος. Plutarch " in Mario.) repassed the Rhine, — acquired a " just title to the name of Cimbri, which signifies " a band of robbers (Κιμβρας επονομαζϖσι Γερμανοι " τϖς λῃςας. Plutarch in Mario. λῃςρικοι οντες " και πλανητες οι Κιμβροι. Strabo, lib. vii.)—, " and,—more than three centuries prior to the " Christian æra,—extended their conquests to— " Great Britain. — And the Welsh retain, in " their name, an undoubted mark of their Cim- " bric extraction."

And in p. 30 thus— " When some of the " Cimbri appeared on the frontiers of Greece, " others drove the ancient Gael from the Belgic

[1] C. 12. 16, and 17.

" division

" division of Gaul—(reperiebat Cæsar Belgas
" esse ortos ab Germanis Rhenum antiquitus transf-
" ductos, propter loci fertilitatem ibi consedisse;
" Gallosque qui ea loca incolerent, expulisse.
" lib. ii.)."

I have brought these two passages together, in order to exhibit by both the whole of Mr. Macpherson's assertions and authorities upon this subject. Mr. Macpherson frequently goes over the same points again in the progress of his disquisition, and very strangely neglects to give authorities for his assertions in the first instance, but produces them in the second. And the three great particulars contained in the extracts are these, That the German Celtæ repassed the Rhine more than 300 or (p 28) about 270 years before Christ; That the name of Cimbri was peculiarly given on occasion of this expedition into Gaul; and, That Cymri, the indigenous appellation of the Welsh at present, is a full proof of the German Celtæ having passed over in a large colony into Britain. Each shall be the subject of a distinct paragraph.

That the German Celtæ repassed the Rhine into Gaul at the one or the other of the periods mentioned above, is the first point in Mr. Macpherson's deduction of his second colony into Britain. It was this which gave the first motion to the great mass of matter on the continent, and occasioned those vibrations that were so fen-

sibly

sibly felt into the island. And yet, by a strange unhappiness, the alledged fact does not carry the smallest appearance of a proof where it is first mentioned, and carries only the appearance of one where it is mentioned again. The four first quotations are not intended to authenticate the fact at all. Two of them only assert the Gauls to have been denominated Cimbri, and the others only intimate the Cimbri of Germany to have been actually robbers. But none of the four in the least asserts the remigration of the German Celtæ into Gaul at this period. And in p. 30 the only authority for the fact is the passage from Cæsar, which runs thus in the original: Reperiebat plerosque Belgas esse ortos a Germanis; Rhenumque antiquitus transductos, propter loci fertilitatem ibi confedisse; Gallosque qui ea loca incolerent expulisse. But this is no proof, any more than the quotations before, that the German Celtæ repassed the Rhine at this period under the name of Cimbri. It shews not the Belgæ to have been German Celtæ at all. It shews not the Belgæ to have been ever denominated Cimbri. And it shews them not to have repassed the Rhine either 300 or 270 years before Christ. The Belgæ indeed crossed the Rhine into Gaul many years before either of these periods, since they penetrated into Britain, as I shall shew hereafter, no less than 350 years before Christ. And the Belgæ certainly were not

the

the people, that Mr. Macpherson here intimates them to have been, and that they must have been if they were the same with Mr. Macpherson's Cimbri. The Belgæ never " ravaged all " the regions lying between the Rhine and the " Ionian sea," never " poured irresistible armies " into Greece, Thrace, and Macedonia," never " cut to pieces all the intermediate nations be-" tween their original seats and the Hellespont," never " filled the lesser Asia with their colonies," and never " extended their conquests into Spain." These magnificent actions are attributed before to the German Celtæ in general, under the name of Cimbri. They are now attributed to that body of the Germans which was particularly denominated Belgæ. And I have previously demonstrated that they belonged to neither, but were wholly the exploits of the Native Gauls or Proper Celtæ.

Nor was the name of Cimbri given to the Belgæ, on occasion of their expedition back into Gaul. That the Belgæ ever bore the appellation, has not yet been proved by Mr. Macpherson. And it was never the mere appropriated title of the German Celtæ in general, or of any division of them in particular. It was the general and common denomination of the whole collective body of the Celtæ. And such it appears very early on the continent. The natives and residents of Gaul, that I have previously shewn to
have

have broke into Greece, to have attacked Delphi, and to have ravaged Afia, thefe appear to have been denominated equally Galli, Celtæ, Cimmerii, or Cimbri. The Celtæ, who are called Cimbri, fays Appian, encamped againſt Delphi: Κελτοις, τοις λεγομενοις Κιμβροις, επι Δελφοις συςρατευσαι [1]. Speaking of the Teutones and Cimbri, Plutarch fays that the Cimmerii were firſt known to the Greeks in former ages, Κιμμεριων το μεν πρωτον υφ' Ελληνων των παλαι γνωσθεντων [2]. The Gauls, fays Diodorus, who in antient times overran all Afia, were denominated Cimmerii: εν τοις παλαιοις χρονοις της Ασιαν απασαν καταδραμοντας, ονομαζομενες δε Κιμμεριας [3]. And the Galatæ of the Greeks, fays Joſephus, were formerly called Gomarians; τες μεν νυν υφ' Ελληνων Γαλατας καλεμενες, Γομαρεις λεγομενες [4]. The Celtæ of Germany therefore muſt, equally with the Celtæ of Greece and Afia, have carried the name into all the countries that they conquered. And it was not any appropriated diſtinction of the Celtæ in Germany or in Greece

---

[1] P. 1196. Amſtel. [2] Vol. ii. p. 495.
[3] P. 355.
[4] Ant. lib. i. c. 7. And, in confirmation of this paſſage of Joſephus, Mr. Pezron has very juſtly remarked, that feveral others of the antients have aſſerted the fame, Euſtathius of Antioch in his, Γαμιροςις Γαμαρεις, της νυν Γαλατας, συνεςησεν— Jerom in his, Sunt autem Gomer, Galatæ—and Iſidore in his, Gomer, ex quo Galatæ, id eſt, Galli.

from

from the Celtæ in Gaul. It was the standing signature of the original derivation of both from the stock of the Cimmerii in Gaul. And it was obviously the first and original characteristic of that great national family, which was afterwards denominated Galli and Celtæ. Distinguished by the epithets of Galli and Celtæ from their mode and manner of living, as I shall shew hereafter; they must naturally have been distinguished before by some primæval and family appellation, by something that carried the note of their descent from the great patriarch of their line. And such appears to be the name of Cimmerii. Variously written Cimbri, Cimmerii, Cumri, Gumri, and Gomerite, it bears all the marks of an original and hereditary signature, and points fully, as it is expresly referred by history[1], to the patriarch Gomer. — The name therefore did not commence about three centuries before Christ. It had been a name for ages before that period. The denomination was not given to the German Celtæ by the Gauls, for their re-entrance into Gaul at that period, and as a mark of ignominy for their devastations in it. It was at that time the hereditary denomination of the Gauls themselves. And the appellation was not borne by the Belgæ, or any or all of the German

---

[1] Josephus Ant. lib. i. c. 7. The name is written Gumri by Llowarch Hên. in the sixth century; see Lhuyd's Archæol.

Celtæ, as the appropriated name of the Germans; becaufe it was borne equally by the Gauls of Greece, the Gauls of Macedonia, and the Gauls of Afia, and was the one comprehenfive title of all.

This directly accounts for the difcovery of the fame name in Britain, without calling in the extravagant and unwarranted fuppofition, that the Celtæ of North-Germany fettled in the ifland. That this fuppofition is void of any fupport in hiftory, is obvious from the management of Mr. Macpherfon himfelf, who grounds it only on the name. "The Welfh," he fays p. 13, " re-" tain in their name an undoubted mark of their " Cimbric extraction." " In Britain," he fays p. 30, " their very name remains, with their " blood, in the Cimbri of Wales." But I have already fhewn the name to have not been the appropriated appellation of the German Celtæ, but the one univerfal title of the Gallic, the German, the Græcian, and the Afiatic Gauls. The fixed indigenous denomination of the Gauls at home, it was carried with their colonies into the Eaft, into Germany, and into Britain. The fixed indigenous appellation of the Gauls abroad, it was retained by them, equally as the general title of all and as the particular defignation of fome. Thus one third of the Gael on the Continent was particutarly denominated Galli, and one third of the Celtæ in Gaul was diftinctively denominated

nominated Celtæ, in the days of Cæsar[1]. And the Gauls of Asia Minor were called Cimmerians, or Gomerites, in the days of Josephus [2]. Thus, when all the German Celtæ were denominated Cimbri or Cambri, there was a nation of Si-Cambri upon the banks of the Rhine, and a tribe of Cimbri within the peninsula of Jutland [3]. And thus the common appellation of all the tribes of Britain, is still retained by the descendants of three of them in Wales. The Welsh therefore preserve no mark of their extraction from the German Celtæ, in their present denomination of Cymri. It is the sign only of their original derivation from the Cimmerii of Gaul. And Mr. Macpherson's whole scheme, of a Cimbric or Celto-Germanic establishment in the island, appears to be entirely hypothetical and groundless.

P. 12, 13. " The first irruption of the nations
" of the Northern Germany happened, as we
" have already observed, more than three cen-
" turies before the commencement of our present
" æra. About two ages after, the Celtæ beyond
" the Rhine threw another fleece of adventurers,

---

[1] P. 1.   [2] Ant. lib. i. c. 7.
[3] History of Manchester, p. 427.

" under

"under the name of Cimbri, into the regions of
"the South (Sexcentefimum & quadragefimum
"annum urbs noftra agebat cùm Cimbrorum
"audita funt arma. Tacit. Germ. 37.)."

I have produced this extract, merely to point out, how unfriendly and hoftile Mr. Macpherfon's own quotations would be to his fyftem, if they were not a little garbled by him. — Of the two irruptions here afferted, the authority adduced for the latter entirely precludes the former. The paffage is crippled in Mr. Macpherfon's quotation. In the original it runs thus. Proximi Oceano Cimbri, parva nunc civitas, fed gloria ingens —. Sexcentefimum et quadragefimum annum urbs noftra agebat, cùm *primùm* Cimbrorum audita funt arma. This therefore was the firft irruption of the Cimbri into the South of Europe. And Mr. Macpherfon's own quotation, when it is reftored to its original perfection, exprefsly declares it to have been the firft.

These are all the parts of Mr. Macpherfon's great argument in favour of a German-Celtic colony fettling in the ifland. And every part, we fee, afferts fome fact that is not true, or deduces

duces some reasoning that is not just. The whole therefore is one system of Error. And the existence of a second colony in Britain, as distinct from the Gael of the first and the Belgæ of the second, appears to be totally ungrounded. In all the arguments but one, Mr. Macpherson has confounded the German with the Proper Celtæ, though the very scope and purpose of his arguments necessarily led him to distinguish accurately between them. And in that one Mr. Macpherson has confounded the Cimbri with the Belgæ. Having accompanied the German Celtæ, or the Cimbri, in all their imaginary expeditions across the continent of Europe, we find them at last dwindled down into the Belgæ, who had never been mentioned before, and to whom the preceding quotations, even as interpolated and garbled by Mr. Macpherson's own inadvertency and prejudice, have not the smallest reference. Having through various pages engaged the Germans in incursions which they never made, and in ravages which they never committed, Mr. Macpherson at last attributes them to a small body of the Germans, the Belgæ, whose only incursion was from the German to the Gallic side of the Rhine, and whose only ravages were confined to a corner of Gaul. And the whole account, as the reader must already have observed, is supported by a train of the

most

moſt extraordinary inaccuracies, involuntary miſquotations, unintended perverſions, and miſtaken reaſonings, that perhaps ever occurred within ſo ſhort a compaſs, in the writings of a man of learning, taſte, and diſcernment.

III.

CONCERNING THE THIRD COLONY THAT MR. MACPHERSON BRINGS INTO BRITAIN.

PAG. 31. " The Cimbri who remained in
" Gaul became [came] afterwards [after
" the paſſage of others into Britain] to be diſtin-
" guiſhed by the name of Belgæ. As that ap-
" pellation carries reproach in its meaning, it is
" likely that it was impoſed on that warlike
" nation by the Gael whom they had expelled
" from

"from their territories. Balge or Balgen, in
"the ancient Celtic fignified a fpotted or party-
"coloured herd, and, in a metaphorical fenfe,
"a mixed people, or an aggregate of many
"tribes. The name alludes either to Belgium's
"being peopled promifcuoufly by the German
"tribes, or to the unavoidable mixture of the
"Celtic colonies beyond the Rhine with the
"Sarmatæ of the Eaft and North."

We are told before, in p. 10, "that the German
"Celtæ re-paffed the Rhine, committed terrible
"devaftations, and acquired a juft title to the
"name of Cimbri, which fignifies a band of
"robbers." And we are here told, that the
Cimbri were diftinguifhed in Gaul by the name
of Belgæ. The Gael, that had been expelled
from their own territories, muft have been the
perfons that gave them the appellation of Cimbri
or Robbers. And yet they are here reprefented
as giving them the name of Belgæ. The former
was a ftrong brand upon their national character,
and a lively mark of the refentment of the
injured Gael. And yet it is here fuppofed to have
been fuperfeded foon afterwards by a title from
the fame injured people, that carries little or no
reproach with it. — But this derivation of the
names of Cimbri and Belgæ is all as imaginary,
as the refting a momentous point of hiftory
upon fuch precarious deductions is weak and
trifling. The German Celtæ, as I have fhewed
before,

before, must necessarily have carried the name of Cimbri with them across the Rhine into Germany, and have brought it with them into Gaul again. And the name of Belgæ appears not to have been given in Gaul, and seems to have been borne in Germany. Cæsar says, plerosque Belgas esse ortos a Germanis, Rhenumque antiquitus transductos—ibi consedisse, Gallosque — expulisse: where we have not the least intimation of any change in the name upon their passing into Gaul, and where they seem to have borne the same appellation on the German as on the Gallic side of the Rhine. And, wherever it was given or assumed, it was certainly no title of reproach, because the Belgæ appear universally acknowledging it for their own on the Continent, in Britain, and in Ireland. This therefore entirely sets aside the indistinct and forced etymology of Mr. Macpherson, because it carries a reproach in its meaning. And the name must be derived from some principle of distinction, that was admitted by the Belgæ as well as their neighbours, and will adapt itself to their condition either in Germany or in Gaul. The Belgæ pretty certainly lived, before their migration into Gaul, immediately on the German side of the Rhine. And as they and their neighbours must have been all equally Celtic [1], the name

---

[1] See hereafter for the Belgæ.

must

muſt have been derived from the Celtic language. They were a large aſſociation of tribes in Gaul, and muſt therefore have been the ſame in Germany ¹. They had ſeized no leſs than one third of all Gaul ² : And they muſt therefore have been very conſiderable for their power in Germany. And the name of Belg ſeems to have been highly characteriſtic of their greatneſs, as Balc in Iriſh ſignifies Strong or Mighty. This Etymon at leaſt does not, like Mr. Macpherſon's, violate any proprieties of criticiſm. It confronts no evidence of records. And it is not made either the buttreſs or the baſis of any viſionary ſyſtem in hiſtory.

P. 32, 33. "The Celto-Germanic tribes, who
" had driven the old Gael from Belgium, ſettling
" in that diviſion of Gaul, roſe, in proceſs of
" time, into a variety of petty ſtates. Each of
" theſe, ſome time before the arrival of Cæſar,
" ſent colonies into Britain.—It is difficult to
" aſcertain the æra of this third migration from
" the continent."

The Belgæ are aſſerted by Mr. Macpherſon to have made two migrations into Britain, and to have ſettled two colonies in the iſland, one

¹ Cæſar p. 34.   ² Cæſar p. 1.

under

under the name of Cimbri, and the other under the appellation of Belgæ. The existence of the former incident I have already demonstrated to be merely visionary. But the latter is real. Mr. Macpherson however, in dividing one migration and one colony into two, has even thrown an air of fiction and falsity over the truth.

As the Belgæ were broken into various tribes when they crossed the Rhine, they must already have formed a variety of petty states. And this is confirmed by Cæsar's account of them. When he enquired of the Rhemi concerning their neighbours the Belgæ, quæ civitates, quantæque in armis essent, et quid in bello possent, sic reperiebat, plerosque Belgas esse ortos a Germanis, that most of their civitates or tribes were derived from Germany, the Bellovaci, the Suessiones, the Nervii, and the Attrebates, the Ambiani, the Morini, the Menapii, and the Caletes, the Velocasses, the Veromandui, and the Atuatici; and that the other states were native Germans, Condrusos, Eburones, Cæraesos, Pœmanos, qui uno nomine Germani appellantur[1]. There was no need therefore of any interval of time after the invasion of Gaul by the Belgæ, to reduce them into various states. Already reduced, they therefore ranged as distinct tribes in Germany, and therefore settled as distinct

[1] P. 33 and 34.

communities

communities in Gaul. Nor did each of these states send colonies into Britain. The number of Belgic communities in Gaul was 12. And the number of Belgic colonies in Britain was only 5. These were the Cantii of Kent, the Regni of Sussex, the Proper Belgæ of Hampshire and Wiltshire, the Durotriges of Dorsetshire, and the Damnonii of Devonshire. And these afterwards planted a new colony, under the name of Trinovantes, in the counties of Middlesex and Essex.

P. 33. "It is difficult to ascertain the æra of
" this third migration from the continent. We
" ought to place it perhaps half a century prior
" to the arrival of Cæsar. Divitiacus, King of
" the Suessiones, who flourished before that
" great commander, may probably have trans-
" planted from Gaul those tribes in Britain over
" whom he reigned."

When the Belgæ made their imaginary migration into Britain, under the name of Cimbri, about three centuries before Christ, they are supposed to have passed over into the island immediately after their arrival in Gaul. "Descrying, from their new settlements, the island
" of Britain, they passed the narrow channel
" which divides it from the continent [1]." Their

[1] P. 30.

second

second migration into Britain, under the name of Belgæ, is pushed two centuries lower, in order to make it distinct and separate from the other. But as they only made one of these expeditions into the island, so this was begun as early as 3½ centuries before Christ. That invaluable collector of antient notices, Richard of Cirencester, here throws a remarkable light upon the dark period of the British history. A. M. 3650. Has terras intrârunt Belgæ—and, Ejecti a Belgis Britones [1]. And the Belgæ were certainly not transplanted by Divitiacus into Britain. They had been settled about 250 years in the island, when Divitiacus came over into it. Apud Suessiones, says Cæsar, fuisse regem nostrâ etiam memoriâ Divitiacum, totius Galliæ potentissimum, qui, quum magnæ partis harum regionum, tum etiam Britanniæ, imperium obtinuerit [2]. He acquired the sovereignty of the continental and the island Belgæ. And, bringing over a large reinforcement of the former, he enabled the latter to extend their possessions into the interiour regions of the country. Cum exercitu in hoc regnum transiit Rex Æduorum [Suessionum] Divitiacus, magnamque ejus partem subegit [3]. The possessions of the Belgæ, before the coming of Divitiacus, in all probability ex-

[1] P. 50.   P. 34.   [3] P. 50.

tended

tended, as I have shewn already in the History of Manchester, over Kent and a small part of Middlesex, over Sussex, and the greatest part of Hampshire and Wiltshire, over Dorsetshire, Devonshire, and a part of Cornwall. And he subdued the rest of Middlesex, and all Essex, all Surrey, the rest of Hampshire, and the adjoining parts of Berkshire, the rest of Wiltshire, the remainder of Cornwall, all Somersetshire, and the South-West of Gloucestershire¹.—The æra of the Belgic migration into Britain then is here ascertained, and shewn to have been, not " half " a century," but three centuries, " prior to the " arrival of Cæsar." And Divitiacus is shewn not to " have transplanted from Gaul those tribes in " Britain over whom he reigned," but only to have brought over an army, and to have only made some additions to the previous possessions of the Belgæ.

This is the short sum of Mr. Macpherson's arguments for a third colony in Britain. As the proof of a colony of Belgæ in the inland, the ar-

---

¹ History of Manchester, p. 60, 61, and 412, 413.

gument carries every conviction with it. But as the proof of a third colony, as a proof that the Belgæ first settled in Britain under their own name about a century only before Christ, it is equally erroneous and trifling.

CHAP.

CHAP. II.

THUS far I have attended minutely to the motions of Mr. Macpherson's Celtæ on the continent. I have demonstrated his account of them, I think, to be one gross perversion of the real history. And I shall now follow him into the island. By disproving the incidents and reasonings, from which he deduces the origin of three colonies in Britain, I have disproved the existence of them already. But I shall still pursue him through all his reasonings and facts in the island, and endeavour to unravel the one and to overthrow the other, with the same respect to Mr. Macpherson, and with the same fidelity to truth.

I.

CONCERNING THE POSITION, MANNERS, AND TRANSACTIONS OF MR. MACPHERSON'S THREE COLONIES IN BRITAIN.

PAG. 32. "When the Romans carried their "arms into Britain, the whole island was "possessed by three nations sprung originally, "though at very different periods, from the Gael "of the continent."

Let us examine this position by the account of him, who was the first Roman that carried his arms into Britain, and who is the most accurate distinguisher of the general divisions of the Britons. Britanniæ pars interior, he says, ab iis incolitur, quos natos in insulâ ipsâ *memoriâ proditum* dicunt: maritima pars ab iis qui — ex Belgis transierant[1]. Here we see the island, not partitioned, like Gaul, into three divisions, but

[1] Cæsar, p. 8⁵,

broken only into two. Here we see the islanders, not divided, as Mr. Macpherson has divided them, into Gael, Cimbri, and Belgæ; but distinguished merely into Belgæ and Aborigines. The Belgæ were known to have passed lately and recently from the continent, in comparison with the Aborigines, though they came 300 years before Cæsar. And the Aborigines had been all of them many ages before, all of them immemorially, settled in the island. The assertion of Mr. Macpherson, therefore, is directly in the face of history. And, when the Romans carried their arms into Britain, the whole country was possessed only by two great divisions of people.

— " The Cimbri, — retiring from the pressure of these new invaders [the Belgæ], possessed the country to the West of the Severne, and that which extended from the Humber to the Tweed. The Gael, under the general name of Caledonians, inhabited the rest of the island to the extremity of the North."

The whole southern region of the island, from the British Channel to the Humber and from the Severne to the German ocean, is here consigned over to the Belgæ. And this is done, equally without any pretence of authority, and in direct opposition to proof. Any person, that has the least acquaintance with the interior disposition of the island in the time of the Britons, must know this

this to be utterly falfe. Cæfar, as I have quoted him immediately above, exprefsly afferts the Belgæ to have been confined to the fouthern coaft. Britanniæ *pars interior* ab iis quos natos in infulâ ipsâ memoriâ proditum dicunt: *Maritima pars ab iis qui — ex Belgis tranfierant.* And fo far were the Belgæ from advancing their poffeffions up to the Humber, that they actually carried them very little beyond the Thames[1]. Thus unhappy is Mr. Macpherfon in every ftep that he takes, on his entrance upon the Interior Hiftory of Britain.

P. 33, 34. "This fuperior civilization [of " the Belgæ] rendered them objects of depreda- " tion to the Cimbri —. They made frequent in- " curfions into the Belgic dominions; and it was " from that circumftance that the Cimbri be- " yond the Humber derived their name of Bri- " gantes, which fignifies a race of freebooters " and plunderers (On lui donna ce nom à caufe " des pillages qu'il faifoit fur les terres de fes " voifins. BRIGAND ou BRIGANT, Brigand, " Pillard, Voleur de Grand-Chemin. Bullet " Memoires fur la lang. Celt. tom. i.)."[2]

[1] See Hiftory of Manchefter, p. 412, 413.
[2] So in Dr. Macpherfon the Brigantes are interpreted Robbers, p. 112.

The

The only reason, for Mr. Macpherson's fixing the Cimbri between the Humber and the Tweed, as well as in Wales, was obviously the antient and present appellation of Cumberland in one part of it. And the only ground, for Mr. Macpherson's asserting the incursions of the Cimbri into the dominions of the Belgæ, was the appellation of Brigantes in another. Upon such slight springs does the vast machine of this history move. But, as the Belgæ never extended their possessions to the Humber, the Cimbri beyond it could not possibly make incursions into them. And, even if they could, as those invasions were made equally by their brethren of Wales as by them, their brethren must equally with them have obtained the opprobrious appellation of Brigantes.

But the Brigantes were not denominated at all from any incursions to the South of the Humber. They made none that appear in history. Able as we are to discover their expeditions into Lancashire, Westmoreland, Cumberland, Anandale, and Cheshire [1], we have not one trace of any into the counties of Lincoln and Nottingham. And the name was not peculiar to the Britons of Yorkshire and Durham. It was equally the name of some of the Celtic settlers on the Alps [2], of

[1] History of Manchester, p. 8, and 104, 105.
[2] Strabo, p. 316. Amstel. and see p. 190 also.

some of Mr. Macpherson's Belgæ to the South of the Humber, and of all Mr. Macpherson's Gael to the North of the Tweed. Galgacus, a native Briton, calls the Iceni, the Trinovantes, and the Cassii, all that united in the great revolt under Boadicea, by the general name of Brigantes: Brigantes, feminâ duce, exurere coloniam, expugnare castra, &c.¹. And Pausanias, speaking of the whole body of the Caledonians, equally calls them all Brigantes ².

This name then could not possibly be given to the Britons of Yorkshire, because of their frequent incursions to the South of the Humber. They made none. And the name was given equally to others, and even to Mr. Macpherson's own plundered Belgæ. It was in truth the general appellation of the Aboriginal tribes of Britain. The name of Cymri was brought with the first colonists into the island, the hereditary appellation of their ancestors on the continent. But the name of Brigantes was conferred upon them in consequence of their passage into it, and was the natural signature of their separation from their brethren in Gaul ³. And it was therefore the equal appellation of those Celtæ, who had migrated from the rest by crossing the channel

---

¹ Agric. Vit. c. 31.
² History of Manchester, p. 9, 10. and 454.
³ History of Manchester, p. 9, 10.

into Britain, and of those who had sequestered themselves from the rest among the mountains and vallies of the Alps.—Nor was the name of Brigantes confined merely to the Aboriginal tribes of the island. It was extended equally to the communities of the Belgæ within it. The Belgic Trinovantes are included by Galgacus, together with the Iceni and the Cassii, under the general designation of Brigantes. And all the tribes of the Belgæ in Britain were therefore expressly denominated, as a nation on the continent, that was inclosed on three sides from the rest of the Gauls by the Soane and the Rhone, equally was, the Allo-Brog-es, or the sequestered and separated Gauls¹.

It is an obvious truth, but it has been little attended to by the tribe of etymologists from Bochart to Mr. Macpherson, that names descriptive of national manners cannot possibly be the original appellations of any people. They result from the intercourse and experience of the states around them, and are the natural expressions of their passions and feelings. And they must therefore in their own nature, not be primary, but posterior, denominations; not the names under which the nations originally settled in their own possessions, but those which were

¹ See History of Manchester, p. 9, and Cæsar, p. 4 and 6.

imposed

imposed upon them afterwards, when they encroached upon the possessions of others. Hence the name of Brigantes came to signify, on the continent and in the island, a turbulent plundering race of men [1]. Hence the name of Cimbri acquired the same signification in Germany [2]. And thus the names of the Celtic Ambrones and Gael finally sunk into mere words of reproach, and came to import, even among the Celtæ and the Gael of this island, the Ferocious and the Stranger.

P. 32. "The Cimbri — possessed the country to the West of the Severne, and that which extended from the Humber to the Tweed. The Gael, under the general name of Caledonians, inhabited the rest of the island to the extremity of the North."

I have already demonstrated this division of the island to be directly contrary to history, as it respects the Belgæ. I shall now endeavour to prove it equally wrong, as it respects the Cimbri and the Gael.

---

[1] See Strabo, p. 316; and Camden, p. 556. Edit. 1607.
[2] Plutarch, p. 495. vol. ii.
[3] See History of Manchester, p. 429, for Ambrones: and the Irish call a stranger and an enemy Gael at present.

The names of Gael and Cimbri were not appropriated, as our author has apppropriated them from the beginning. Gael was not the diftinguifhing appellation of the Caledonians from the Cimbri and the Belgæ. And Cimbri was not the diftinguifhing appellation of the Welfh and the Brigantes from the Belgæ and the Gael. Mr. Macpherfon's Belgæ were denominated Cimbri, and Mr. Macpherfon's Belgæ and Cimbri were denominated Gael.

I have previoufly fhewn the name of Cymri to have been the great hereditary diftinction of the Gauls upon the continent, and to have been carried with them into all their conquefts. There I have fhewn it to have been retained, equally as the general title of all their tribes, and as the particular defignation of fome. And it was not retained in our own ifland, as Mr. Macpherfon fuppofes, merely by the natives of Wales and the Britons of Brigantia. It was equally the name of a nation in the South-Weft of Somerfetfhire and the North-Eaft of Cornwall. In hoc brachio, quæ [quod] intermiflione Uxellæ amnis Heduorum regioni protenditur, fita eft regio Cimbrorum[1]. And the name appears plainly, not to have been continued as a particular appellation from the beginning, but to have been taken up at different periods by different tribes, even in fuperfedence of their

---

[1] Richard p. 20. and Hiftory of Manchefter, p. 61.

own

own previous appellations, when they wanted to diſtinguiſh themſelves from their enemies around them. Thus the Cimbri of Somerſetſhire and Cornwall were poſſeſt of the appellation before the Romans arrived in the iſland, becauſe they were cloſely ſkirted by their enemies, the Belgæ of Cornwall, Devonſhire, Dorſetſhire, and Somerſetſhire [1]. The Voluntii of Brigantia in the 6th century, when they were preſſed by the Saxons from the Eaſt, laid aſide the appellation by which they had been diſtinguiſhed for ages, and, as the Welſh Cymri is colloquially pronounced Cumri, denominated themſelves Cumbri [2]; and the principal part of their country is called Cumberland at preſent. And the Silures, the Dimetæ, and the Ordovices, of Wales, in the later ages of their Empire, when they were attacked by the Saxons on every ſide, threw off their former appellations entirely, and have ever ſince diſtinguiſhed themſelves by the generical appellation of Cymri.

The names of Cymri and of Gael are both equally the general deſignations of the Celtæ. The former related only to the Patriarch of the

---

[1] Hiſtory of Mancheſter, p. 61, and 413.
[2] Hence Llomarch Hean, a nobleman of Voluntia, and a writer of the 6th century, flying with many others from the Saxons of the North into Shropſhire, calls it the paradiſe of the Cumbrians, Pouys Paraduys Gumri (Lhuyds Archæologia, under Llowarch).

Line;

Line; but the latter, as I shall shew hereafter, to the residence of his posterity among the wilds and woodlands of Gaul. Denominated Gael upon the continent, the colonists continued the name in the island. And it survives not, as Mr. Macpherson uniformly imagines, solely in that name of Gael which the Irish and Highlanders reciprocally give themselves. It survives, as I have shewed before, in the name of Gathel, which is equally pronounced Gael, and was once equally the appellation of the Irish, the Highlanders, and the Welsh. And it survives also in the name of Welsh, the whole body of the Provincials being repeatedly denominated in general Bryt-Walas, Wilsc, or Welsh, in the Saxon Chronicle; the Britons of Kent, the Britons of Sussex, the Britons of Hampshire, the Britons of Dorsetshire, the Britons of Wiltshire, the Britons of Bedfordshire, the Britons of Somersetshire, the Britons of Cheshire, and the Britons of Clydisdale in Scotland, being all distinctly particularized in the Chronicle as Wealas, Walen, or Bryt-Wealas; and the Britons of Galloway, Wales, and Cornwall retaining the appellation at present[1]. These are such obvious

---

[1] See History of Manchester, p. 437.—In p. 1. of the Sax. Chron. the Britons are called British or Wilsh, in p. 2. the Britons that opposed Cæsar's passage over the Thames are called Brytwalas, in p. 7. all the Provincials to the South of Severus's Wall are named Brytwalum, and in p. 11 and 12.

relicks

relicks of the name of Gael, scattered over the whole face of the island, that it is very surprizing Mr. Macpherson should ever have thought of appropriating the name to the Irish and the Highlanders.

The Welsh then, who from their name of Cymri are inferred by Mr. Macpherson to be a distinct colony from the Gael, may with greater reason be inferred from their names of Gathel and of Welsh, to be absolutely the same with them. And the name of Wales, which has been universally affirmed by the English criticks to have been imposed upon the country by the Saxons, and as universally agreed by the Welsh to have been never acknowledged by their countrymen, actually appears the acknowledged appellation of the region as early as the 6th century, and in the poems of a Welsh Bard;

  Eu Ner a folant,
  Eu hiaith a gadwant,
  Eu tir a gollant,
    Ond gwyllt Wallia [1];

actually all the Provincials, all from the Friths to the British Channel, are denominated Brytwalas and Brytwalana. The Welsh of Kent are repeatedly mentioned in p. 14, of Sussex twice in p. 14, of Hampshire p. 15, of Dorsetshire p. 25. (See Carte, p. 226. V. I.), of Wiltshire p. 20, of Bedfordshire p. 22, of Somersetshire p. 39, of Cheshire p. 25, and of Clydisdale p. 83 and 110.

[1] Taliessin, as cited by Mr. Wynne in Gent. Mag. for July

They shall still praise their Maker,
They shall still keep their language,
They shall still be deprived of their lands,
        Except uncultivated Wales.

The Belgæ, who are supposed to be still more distinct, and were actually very different, from the Gael, yet, being equally derived with them from Gaul, bear equally the appellation of Gael; the Belgæ being all denominated in general, like a tribe on the continent of Gaul, Allo-Broges, or the Galli Brigantes, amongst the antients; and the Belgæ of Kent, Sussex, Hampshire, Dorsetshire, Wiltshire, and Somersetshire, being all specifically denominated Weal- as in the Saxon Chronicle. The Cymri and the Belgæ are both denominated Gael, with the Irish and the Highlanders. And Mr. Macpherson's Belgæ I have shewn before to have been also denominated Cimbri, with the Welsh. The name therefore, which Mr. Macpherson selects as the distinguishing mark of his 2d colony from his 1st and 3d, appears to have been common to his 3d and 2d. And the name, which Mr. Macpherson assigns as the sure signature of his 1st, appears to have been familiar to all the three,

---

1770, and also in a Pamphlet on the Welsh language printed a few years ago at Cowbridge in Glamorganshire.

P. 35, 36.—" The three great British Nations, whose origin we have endeavoured to investigate, must have differed considerably from one another in language, manners, and character. Though descended from the same source, their separation into different channels was very remote. The Gael—, having passed from the continent before the arts of civil life had made any considerable progress among them, retained the pure but unimproved language of their ancestors together with their rude simplicity of manners. The British Cimbri derived their origin from the Galic colonies who, in remote antiquity, had settled beyond the Rhine. These, with a small mixture of the Sarmatæ, returned, in all their original barbarism, into the regions of the South. During their separation from their mother nation, their language and manners must have suffered such a considerable change, that it is extremely doubtful whether their dialect of the Celtic and that of the old British Gael were, at the arrival of the former in this island, reciprocally understood by both nations. The third colony differed in every thing from the Gael and Cimbri. Their manners were more humanized; and their tongue, though perhaps corrupted, was more copious. They had left the continent at a period of advanced civility.—But—the radical

" dical words used by all were certainly the
" same."

Are the several parts of this Extract compleatly at unity with themselves? They seem to be a little heterogeneous. We are first told, that the three nations must have differed considerably in their language, and that it is extremely doubtful, whether the Cimbric and the Gaelic were reciprocally understood at first: and yet we are afterwards told, that " the radical " words used by all were certainly the same." The Gael and Cimbri are said to have " differed " considerably in their manners," when they both retained " the rude simplicity of their " ancestors," and " their original barbarism of " manners," " with a small mixture of the Sar- " matæ" adhering to one of them. The Cimbri are said to have returned " in all their original " barbarism" into Gaul; though, " during " their separation from it, their manners must " have suffered a considerable change." They returned only " with a small mixture of the Sar- " matæ" in their manners; and yet the change was " considerable."—And are not the several parts of this Extract in a state of hostility with other passages in the work? The Gael are here represented, as coming over from Gaul " before " the arts of civil life had made any consider- " able progress," and as therefore retaining " the rude simplicity of their ancestors:" and
yet

yet the Cimbri, who came over from Gaul some ages afterward, are represented as arriving here " in a rude barbarity [1]," and " in all their ori- " ginal barbarism." The Gael are brought into Britain, before the arts had made any *con- siderable* progress in Gaul, and consequently after they had made *some*; as also in p. 34 the Gauls appear to have arrived at " some degree of " civilization," before the Gael left them: and yet the Cimbri, who left the continent three ages afterwards, when the arts of civil life must have been considerably advanced, bring with them a rude barbarity of manners. The Cimbri are here wafted into the island in all their ori- ginal barbarism: and yet, before the Cimbri came over, we find that " the domestic improve- " ments" in Gaul " had arrived at some degree " of maturity [2]." In p. 24 the Gauls appear to have arrived at " some degree of civilization," and in p. 8 agriculture in particular appears to have been " prosecuted with vigour and success," before the Gael left the country: and yet the Gael are here said to have retained the rude simplicity of their ancestors; and in p. 47 the Gael, and in p. 33 even the more southerly Cimbri, are both represented as totally ignorant of agriculture.—But let us not scrutinize too nicely.

I have repeatedly shewn the existence of these 3 colonies, in the island, to be all the creation of

[1] P. 33.   [2] P. 10.

Mr.

Mr. Macpherson's prejudices. And that Mr. Macpherson's Gael, Cimbri, and Belgæ differed very little from each other in their language and manners, is very evident. The language of all the three was exactly the same; as is plain to a demonstration from the appearance of the same names of towns, of rivers, and of tribes among all. We have Camulodunum for the name of a fortress among Mr. Macpherson's Cimbri of Yorkshire, and his Belgæ of Essex; Lindum amongst his Belgæ and his Gael; and Venta for the Capital of his Cimbri in Wales, and of his Belgæ in Hampshire and in Norfolk; Urus or Ure, the name of a river in Yorkshire and in Suffolk, and an appellative for a river in the Erse at present[1]; and Alauna, Deva, and Devana, all three, rivers in the country equally of his Gael, his Belgæ, and his Cimbri; Novantes, a tribe of his Belgæ and his Gael; the Damnonii[2] and Cantæ among his Gael, and the Cantii and Damnonii among his Belgæ; and one tribe of his Gael, and two of his Belgæ, equally denominated Carnabii. And the manners of the three were but little different.

Mr. Macpherson himself shall convince us, that there was no great difference. The most humanized of any of the islanders, the Belgæ, are

[1] See Mr. Macpherson, p. 34. a note.

[2] The Damnii of Valentia are called both Damnii and Dumnonii by Ptolemy.

expressly mentioned by Mr. Macpherson, in p. 33, to have arrived to this " pitch of cultiva- " tion," that " they sowed corn, they had fixed " abodes, and some degree of commerce was " carried on in their ports." And, as some of the other Britons equally sowed corn, so all of them had fixed abodes. Interiores plerique, says Cæsar, frumenta non serunt: some of them therefore did. Cæsar also found towns, and exactly the same sort of towns, among the Abo- riginal and the Belgic Britons [1]. And the only difference between the Belgæ and all the other islanders was this, according to Mr. Macpherson himself, that the former carried on *some* commerce from their ports.

Nor was the difference great in itself betwixt the real Britons and the real Belgæ. They both constructed their houses in the same manner, used the same stated pieces of brass or iron bullion for money, had the same fondness for keeping poultry and hares about their houses, and the same aversion to seeing them upon their tables. They both painted their bodies, both threw off their cloaths in the hour of battle, both suffered the hair of their head to grow to a great length, both shaved all but the upper lip, both had wives in common, and both prose- cuted their wars on the same principles. In all

[1] See History of Manchester, p. 467.

these

these particulars, the great and principal strokes in the national character, the Belgæ and the Britons univerfally agreed. Several of the Britons likewife concurred with the Belgæ in their attention to agriculture, and in wearing garments of woolen. And the only diftinction betwixt them was one, which was really no difference of manners at all; that the Britons, being diflodged from all that fide of the ifland which was immediately contiguous to Gaul and Spain, and the only part of it which was vifited by the foreign traders, were no longer able to purfue the commerce which they had previoufly carried on, and were obliged to refign it up to the Belgæ'.

P. 34—37. " SILURES —, Siol, a race of
" men, Urus, the river emphatically, in allufion
" to their fituation beyond the Severne.—
" CANTIUM, Kent, Canti, end of the Ifland.
" TRINOBANTES, Trion-oban, marfhy diftrict;
" the inhabitants of Middlefex and Effex.—
" DOBUNI, Dobh-buini, living on the bank of
" the river; they who of old poffeffed the coun-
" ty of Gloucefter, alluding to their fituation on
" the banks of the Severne. — ORDOVICES,

¹ See Cæfar, p. 88, 89, and Hift. of Manchefter, p. 385.

"Ord-tuavich, northern mountaineers, the in-
"habitants of North Wales."

Before I perused Mr. Macpherson's Dissertation, I was full of expectation, to see the task of British etymology wrested out of the clumsy hands, in which a general ignorance of the Celtic had hitherto placed it. But sanguine expectations are seldom gratified. And perhaps I expected more than knowledge could supply. Mr. Macpherson however appears plainly, I think, to have derived all his knowledge of the Celtic from the view merely of one of its dialects. And he is frequently unhappy, I apprehend, in his application of that. This I have already shewn in the names of Celt, Cimbri, and Brigantes. And I hope to shew it again in the names before us.

Cantium, here resolved into Cant-i, the end of the island, must be formed upon the same principle, as the appellation of the Cantæ in Caledonia, who resided not at the end of the island, but lived along the eastern coast of it, and to the South of the Frith of Dornoch[1] ; and as the present name of Cantire in Scotland, which is still farther from the end of the island, and lies along the western coast. And the word is clearly Cand or Cant, an Head or Prominence of land,

[1] See History of Manchester, p. 411.

and actually appears in Ptolemy's names for the South-Foreland, Cantion or A-Cantion, Promontory or The Promontory [1]. The Cantii and Cantæ equally borrowed their appellation, from their position upon the headlands of their coast. And Cantire literally signifies an Headland.

The division of Trinobantes into Trion-oban must appear very surprizing, when we consider, that the tribe is denominated Novanei or Novantes in the coins of Cunobeline. And the interpretation of it into Marshy District must appear equally wonderful, when we reflect, that it was originally the name of the dry gravelly site of London. The Belgæ of Kent pushed across the Thames, and seized the South of Middlesex, under the title of Novantes or New-comers [2]. This must have happened a considerable period before the descent of Cæsar, as they then formed a powerful kingdom to the North of the Thames [3], and must therefore have then held all the territories that they afterwards possessed in Middlesex and Essex. Upon their irruption into the South of Middlesex, they selected the fine site of the present London, the eminence betwixt the Thames and the Fleetbrook, for the area of

---

[1] See History of Manchester, p. 467.
[2] History of Manchester, p. 60, 62, and 412.
[3] Trinobantes, prope firmissima earum regionum civitas, p. 92.

a fortress; and the town, that was destined to be afterwards the imperial seat of Britain, they called by the local title of Lon-din or the Water-town, and by the national appellation of Tre-Novantum or the fortress of the Novantes [1]. And, as they spread afterwards from London over all Middlesex and Essex, they carried the name of their original town with them, and their appellation of Novantes was lengthened into Trinovantes.

Dobuni, formed of Dobh-buini, and interpreted the residents on a river, means undoubtedly, as it has been always rendered, the men of the valley. They are therefore called Dubni and Duni in the varying denomination of Cogi-Dubnus and Cogi-Dunus [2], Dumni in the appellation of Togi-Dumnus, and actually and expressly Boduni in Dio. All these terms equally signify the Lowlanders. And the concurrence of all in one meaning decisively fixes it.—And Ordovices, here analysed into Ord-tuavich, and translated Northern Mountaineers, I have shewn, I think, to be Ordo-Uices or Ordo-Vices, the Honourable Vices or the Great Huiccii [3]; as in the fifth century we have a British hero popularly de-

---

[1] History of Manchester, p. 412 and 413.
[2] Chichester Inscription, and Tacitus.
[3] History of Manchester, p. 148.

nominated

nominated Eneon Urd, the fame word with Ard, only varied by the pronunciation, and fignifying Eneon the Honourable or Great[1]; and as we have a promontory in Scotland, bearing the equal appellation of Urd and Ord Head at prefent.

The etymon of Silures is evidently deduced from too trifling and remote a circumftance, their bordering upon the Severn in one part, or, as Mr. Macpherfon expreffes himfelf, their refiding beyond it. And the true etymon may perhaps be, S, Il or Ile, Ur, The Great Men. So we have Elgovæ and Selgovæ in Ptolemy, as the name of the fame people. And the Silures had a juft claim to this magnificent appellation, being a very powerful tribe, and having fubdued the Ordovices and Dimetæ of Wales. They appear alfo pretty plainly, though they have never been fufpected, to have once poffeffed the Caffiterides. The principal of thefe iflands is denominated Silura infula by Solinus, as all of them are to this day denominated the Silley Ifles. Richard has applied to the Silures, what Solinus has fpoken of the inhabitants of Silura[2]. And Tacitus evidently carries the poffeffions of the Silures to the Caffiterides, by placing them oppofite to Spain: Silurum colorati vultus, & torti plerumque crines, & *pofitu contra Hifpaniam*, &c.[3].

---

[1] See Carte, vol. i. p. 179. [2] P. 21.
[3] Agric. vit. c. 11.

P. 38. " Alba or Albin, the name of [by] "which the antient Scots, in their native language, have, from all antiquity, diftinguifhed "their own divifion of Britain, feems to be the "fountain from which the Greeks deduced their "Albion. It was natural for the Gael, who "tranfmigrated from the low plains of Belgium, "to call the more elevated land of Britain by a "name expreffive of the face of the country. "Alb or Alp, in the Celtic, fignifies High, and "In, invariably, a country."

That the Gael tranfmigrated from the low plains of Belgium, is a mere affertion without authority; as the ufe of the word Belgium here is abfolutely equivocal. According to Mr. Macpherfon himfelf, they came not from Belgium, modernly fo called, or Holland, but from the "Belgic divifion of Gaul [1]," which reached from the Seine and the Marne to the mouth of the Rhine [2]. And they came undoubtedly from that part of the divifion, which is the neareft to Britain, and from which they could defcry the ifland. Mr. Macpherfon accordingly reprefents the migration of the Gael, to have been " in croffing a "very narrow channel into Britain [3]." The fact therefore, of the Gael paffing over into Britain from the low plains of Belgium, being un-

[1] P. 26. [2] Cæfar, p. 1. [3] P. 26.

grounded

grounded in history and contradictory to reason, the etymology which is founded upon it must necessarily fall with it.—Nor is the etymology just in itself. Inis or In is so far from signifying invariably a country in general, that, I believe, it invariably signifies an island only. In its general acceptation it certainly means only an island. And the etymology of a popular name, which stands in direct opposition to the popular import of the word, must for that very reason be wrong [1].

What then is the derivation of the name of Albion? It is the same, I think, that has been already given in the History of Manchester [2].— Not imposed by the mere ancestors of the Caledonians, as is here insinuated; it was never imposed, assuredly, by any of the residents in the country. As the island regularly rose every morning to the eye of the Gauls that inhabited along the coast of Calais, and as its chalky cliffs glittered continually in the sun, the Gauls must certainly have beheld them, and could not but have given them some appropriate appellation. This, it is obvious, must necessarily have been

---

[1] So in Dr. Macpherson, p. 116, 117, we have the same interpretation of Albion, the same fallacy concerning Belgium, and the same derivation of the first Britons from "the low plains of Belgium."

[2] P. 9.

the case. This we must suppose to have happened, if no name had been transmitted to us that was characteristic of the circumstance. And the coincidence of the reason and the name is a decisive evidence of the fact. As the Gauls beheld the heights appearing on the other side of the water, they naturally distinguished them by a name, that was expressive only of the sensible appearance which they formed to the eye, and called them Alb-ion or Heights. Alb in the singular lengthens into Alb-an, Alb-on, Alb-ain, or Alb-ion in the plural. And we have the same word in the Gallic appellation of the mountains that divide Italy from Gaul. The Alps, some ages before the days of Strabo, were called Albia; and a very high mountain, that terminated the Alps upon one side, was denominated Albius in his time [1]. And, equally some ages before, the Alps were denominated Albia and Alpionia; and in his time there remained two tribes on the mountains, that bore the names of Albiœci and Albienses [2]. The name therefore was the natural Celtic term for heights or eminences. As such, it was applied to the

---

[1] P. 309 and 483, Strabo.

[2] Strabo, p. 309 and 311.—These mountains were not inhabited when Bellovesus crossed them into Italy (Livy, l. v. c. 34): and they were afterwards possessed by many bodies of the Gauls (Strabo, p. 190.).

cliffs

cliffs of Britain and the mountains of Gaul. And, as such, it is retained by the present Highlanders for their own, very mountainous, division of Britain. The first name of the island, then, was given it before the country was inhabited. Had it been given after that period, and from a view " of the face of the country;" derived as the first inhabitants undoubtedly were, across the narrowest part of the channel, from the bold shore of Calais, and so very level, in general, as all the southern part of the island undoubtedly is, they could never have distinguished it by the name of Albion. But accustomed to see it daily from their own shores, and accustomed to call it the Heights, they soon passed over in all probability from mere motives of curiosity, they perhaps stocked some of the nearer woods with wild beasts for their hunting, and ages afterwards formed a regular settlement on the Albion, that they had so long seen, denominated, and visited [1].

P. 39. " The Cimbri — arriving in Belgium, " and descrying Albion, gave it a new name ex- " pressive of the same idea which first suggested

---

[1] The Romans therefore frequently describe Albion as a level country. Mela says, Siciliæ maxime similis, *Plana*, ingens, &c. (l. iii. c. 6.). And Strabo says, ερι δ' η πλεισ η της ηση ΠΕΔΙΑΣ (p. 305).

" the

"the appellation of Albion to the Gael. Com-
"paring the elevated coast of Britain to the fenny
"plains of the Lower Germany, they called it
"BRAIT-AN, a word compounded of Brait High
"and An or In a Country [1]."

The author has again imposed upon himself by the use of the equivocal term, Belgium. And he has even applied it here in a double acceptation. As relating to "the fenny plains of the "Lower Germany," it can mean only Holland. But as the place from which the Cimbri could "descry Albion," and mark "the elevated coast "of Britain," it refers only to Belgic Gaul. Britain may be seen from the cliffs of the latter, but cannot be discerned from the low plains of the former. — Nor is the author quite consistent with himself in this and the preceding account. The name of Britain, we are told, was "ex-"pressive of the same idea which first suggested "the appellation of Albion to the Gael." And yet Albion is said to be "a name expressive of "the *face* of the country," and Britain to be derived from a view of its "elevated *coast*."—But, even if these accounts were consistent, it shews surely a great want of attention, to deduce the name of Albion from the appearance of the country to those who had migrated into it, and the name of Britain from the aspect of the coast to

---

[1] So Dr. Macpherson, p. 333, interprets Britain to signify Hills.

the diftant inhabitants of Gaul. This refers the fecond name to the view of the coaft, which fhould naturally have given birth to the firft; and afcribes the firft to the face of the country, which fhould as naturally have been the caufe of the fecond. This lets the Gael, who muft have feen the cliffs of the ifland for ages, totally overlook the denominating appearance of it to the eye; and yet forces it afterwards upon the Cimbri. And this fixes not a name upon the country before it was inhabited, though its appearance muft neceffarily have compelled a name fome ages before; and afterwards fetches a name from its appearance, when it had now been inhabited for ages, and when it had already acquired a name from its nature.—But it feems to fhew fomething worfe than inattention, to give neither the Gael nor the Cimbri any other ideas of a country than merely the marfhes of Holland, to attribute the name of Albion to the Gael and of Britain to the Cimbri, to have the former appellation impofed after their fettlement in the country, and to have the latter affixed before their migration into it; and to advance all this without one fingle argument or authority, real or pretended.—I proceed, however, to the etymology itfelf.

In the Hiftory of Manchefter I have fhewn from Pliny, that Britain was not the peculiar

and

and appropriate name of Albion ¹. It was common to all the iflands about it. Albion ipfi nomen fuit, cum Britanniæ vocarentur omnes ². And Mr. Macpherfon's etymology is overthrown at the firft onfet.—In the Hiftory of Manchefter I have equally fhewn from Richard, that Britain was not the name of the ifland originally ³. It was the appellation of the iflanders. Vocabulo gentis fuæ Britanniam cognominaverunt ⁴. And Mr. Macpherfon's etymology is again overthrown.

The real etymon feems to be what is propofed in the Hiftory of Manchefter ⁵. Perhaps I am partial to it as my own. And I will therefore endeavour to open it more fully, and to examine it more attentively, than I did before.

Albion is obvioufly derived from the view of the coaft, before it had been vifited from the continent. Britain therefore, as the fecondary name, was undoubtedly affixed to the country at or after the firft migration into it. While it was only feen from the fhores of Gaul, the name of Albion muft have continued, as the moft natural denomination of the country. And when it came to be fettled, when a body of Gauls had actually migrated acrofs the fea with their wives and children into it, they would ftill ufe the name

---

¹ P. 9. ² L. iv. c. 16. And Ptolemy accordingly calls Ireland and Albion equally a Britifh ifland. ³ P. 9.
⁴ P. 1. And Ifidore fays the fame. ⁵ P. 9—10.

for the country which they had used for ages before in Gaul; and Albion accordingly remained the regular appellation of the island. But the new colonists would naturally be distinguished, among their brethren and themselves, by some denomination expressive of their remove across the Channel, and of their separation from the great body of their countrymen in Gaul. The idea, of their disjunction from Gaul, would naturally be the first that would present itself to the mind. And the idea, of our separation from the continent of Europe, always appears a leading one in the language of the antients concerning us. This then must naturally have vented itself in some appellation of disjunction, for the colonists that crossed the Channel into Britain. And they could scarcely avoid calling themselves, and being called by their brethren, the Separated or Divided Persons. An etymon therefore, expressive of this idea, must be the first that is sought for by a judicious enquirer into the meaning of Britain. And any easy etymology, that is expressive of this idea, must for that reason be superior to every other. Such is the etymology, that is offered in the History of Manchester.

The primitive and radical word in the name of Britain, is obviously Brit. One of our islanders is repeatedly denominated Brit-o and Britt-us by by the Romans, and Bryt by the Saxons [1]. This then is the original word. And this is the very word which Mr. Camden has equally felected, but interpreted to fignify Painted, and to allude to the well-known cuftom of the Britons.—Appellations defcriptive of manners, as I have previoufly obferved, are never the firft and primary defignations of any people. They are the refult of attention to them, and the confequence of obfervations upon them. And long before the untutored and unreflecting mind could catch the characteriftic quality of a people, it muft of courfe have taken up with fome fenfible and exterior difcrimination of them. And where one nation migrated immediately from another, as the Britons from the Gauls, and where the new colonifts could have no communication for ages with any but their brethren in Gaul, there no names characteriftic of manners could poffibly arife. Having no diffimilarity of manners, they could not poffibly diftinguifh each other by it. And the Britons muft have brought the cuftom of painting, as well as all their other cuftoms, originally with them from Gaul.—Nor does Brith properly fignify Painted. This is merely the pofterior and

[1] In Stukeley's Caraufius, V. I. p. 268, we have two Roman Infcriptions, found on the banks of the Rhine, and addreffed Matribus Brittis. And fee Saxon Chronicle, p. 15, &c.

derivative

derivative fignification of the word. It is Brith in Welfh, Brit in Irifh, and Breact[1], Breac, and Bryk, in Erfe, Irifh, and Welfh; and primarily meant any thing Divided. This is evident from the prefent meaning of the word in many of its derivatives, in the Irifh Brioth a Fraction, Brath a Fragment, and Bracaim to break afunder, in the Scotch Bris a Rupture, and in the Welfh Breg a Breach, Bradwy a Fracture, Briw a Fragment, Briwo to break into fragments, and Bradwyog and Brwyd Broken[2]. Carrying with it originally the fingle idea of divifion, it was afterwards, by the natural affimilation of ideas in the human mind, applied to every thing that prefented the idea of a divifion. It was firft applied probably, as in the Irifh and Highland Breacan, to the ftriped mantles of plaid. And, from the colours in regular divifions upon the plaids, it was transferred to objects that were but difperfedly marked with colours; and Brith, Brit, Breact, Breac, and Bryk came to fignify Particoloured, Speckled, and Spotted. Thus Breac ftands for any thing fpeckled or a Trout, Breicin for a fmall Trout, Britineach or Brittinnios for the Meazles, in the Irifh at prefent; Brech is ap-

[1] Offian, V. I. p. 210. a note.

[2] So alfo in the Welfh, Breichio, to take part with any one, Brau and Breuol, Frangible, and Breuolaeth and Breuawd, Frangibility, and in our Anglo-Britifh word Brittle or Frangible.

plied

plied to the Small Pox in Armoric; and Breok, Brethal, Brethil, or Brethel, are used for a Mackerel, Brethyl for a Trout, and Brag-ado for a pied ox, in the Manks, the Cornish, the Armoric, the Welsh, and the Mountain Spanish. And hence it came to signify a Painted object, but such an one only as was coloured merely by parts. This deduction plainly evinces the original and primary idea of the word, and shows from the current meaning of it in all its derivatives, and from the regular analogy of all languages, that it could never have signified Painting, if it had not first imported a Division. This then is the true meaning of the word Brit. And it leads us directly to the natural appellation of a people, that had migrated from their brethren, and were divided from them by the sea.

The original word appears above to have been equally pronounced Brict, Brit, and Brioth, Breact, Breac, and Brig; and appears from the Gallic Brefche a Rupture, the Irish Bris to Break and Brisead a Breach, the Welsh Briwsion Fragments, and the Armorican Breizell, as well as Brethel, a Mackerel, to have been sometimes softened into Bris or Breis. And the word occurs with all this variety of terminations in the Irish Breattain or Breatin, Britain, and in Breathnach, Briotnach, and Breagnach, a Briton; in the Armorican names of Breton,
Breiz,

Breiz, and Brezonnec, for an individual, the country, and the language, of Armorica; in the Welsh Brython and Brythoneg, the Britons, and their language; and in the antient synonimous appellations of Brigantes and Britanni. These I have previously shewn to be synonimous, by demonstrating the Britons all over the island to have been, equally with the Britons of Yorkshire and Durham, denominated Brigantes as well as Britanni. And in the History of Manchester I have shewn the Brigantes of those two counties, to have been peculiarly denominated Britanni also [1].

The national appellation of Brit therefore imports, not the insular nature of Albion, by which it was separated from all the world, but merely its disjunction from Gaul. The former could not be known for ages after the name must have been imposed. And the latter was an obvious and striking particularity. The Gael or Wealas of the continent passing over into Albion, they would naturally be denominated, as they are actually and repeatedly denominated in the Saxon Chronicle, the Bryt-Wealas or the Bryttas [2]. But how shall we lengthen Brit into Britanni and Britones? We cannot with

[1] P. 10.   [2] See p. 2. and 18, &c.   And the sea, which they passed over into this island, appears upon the same principle to have been called by the Britons, for ages afterward, Muir Ict, or the Great Separation. See Usher, p. 429. Edit. 1687.

Camden call in the Greek ταινια, for a country, to our aid. And we muſt not with Pezron and Carte adopt the equivalent Tain of the Celtic. The name of Britain, as I have ſhewn above, was the appellation of the iſlanders, before it was the denomination of the iſland. And the want of attention to the Genius of the Britiſh language has created all the difficulty. It inſtantly vaniſhes, the moment we remark the manner in which the Britiſh words ſhoot out in the Plural. Brict or Brit is enlarged into Brit-on or Brit-an, and therefore, in the antient and modern uſe of the word, is ſometimes Brits [1], Bracht, Brecht [2], and Britt-i, in the Plural, but more commonly Bryth-on; Brit-on-es, and Brit-ann-i, and, in the relative adjectives, Brit-iſh, Breathn-ach, Briotn-ach, Brython-eg, and Brit-ann-ic-i. And the equivalent Brag or Brig is formed, on the ſame principles, into Brig-an or Brig-ant in the Plural, and therefore appears ſometimes as Brig-as, and Brog-es, ſometimes as Breag-n, and Brig-ian-i [4], but generally Brig-ant-es, and, in the relative adjectives, Breagn-ach and Brig-ant-ic [3].

This is a plain and obvious derivation of the name of Britain. It reſults from that ſtriking

[1] Camden, p. 20.   [2] Carte, V. I. p. 25. a note.
[3] Stephanus Byzantinus Lugd. Bat. 1694, p. 245, and Hiſtory of Mancheſter, p. 9.   [4] Pliny, lib. iii. c. 20.

peculiarity

peculiarity in the pofition of the natives, which muſt neceſſarily have denominated the new coloniſts of Albion. And it is deduced from no foreign language, which could not poſſibly have any relation to the name, but flows natural and eaſy from the Celtic.

P. 39. " This new name [Britain] never ex
" tended itſelf to the Gael of North Britain;
" and the poſterity of the Cimbri have loſt it in
" the progreſs of time. The Scottiſh and Iriſh
" Gael have brought down the name of Alba or
" Albin to the preſent age: the Welſh uſe no
" general appellation. The æra of its impoſition
" ought to be fixed as far back as the arrival of
" the Cimbri in the iſland."

In the paragraph immediately preceding this, the name of Britain was impoſed upon the iſland when the Cimbri were yet in Gaul, and before they migrated into Britain. " The Cimbri —,
" arriving in Belgium, and deſcrying Albion,
" gave it a new name —, comparing the elevated
" coaſt of Britain to the fenny plains of the Lower
" Germany." But it is here fixed after the Cimbri had for ſome time beheld the high lands of Albion, after they had left Gaul, and even after they had arrived in the iſland. " The
" æra of its impoſition ought to be fixed as far
" back

"back as the arrival of the Cimbri in the island." How contradictory is this!

And that the name of Britain never extended itself to the Gael of North Britain, and is lost among the Cimbri; and that the name of Albion is the only one, which has been brought down to the present age by the Scottish and Irish Gael; are all gross mistakes, mistakes too in facts where one would least expect them, from a gentleman so conversant in the Celtic language, who speaks the Erse as a native, and has studied it as a critick. With regard to the Irish and Scottish Gael, the reverse of Mr. Macpherson's assertion is the real truth. They have brought down the name of Britain to the present age. And they have not brought down the name of Albion. They retain indeed Alban or Albain for the appellation of their own country: but they are totally ignorant of it as the name of the whole island. And I have shewn before, that the appellatives Britain and Britannic still continue in the Erse, the common language of the Scotch and the Irish, and in the words Breattain, Breatin, Breatnach, and Briotnach. Nor is the name lost among the Welsh, the only part of Mr. Macpherson's Cimbri that speak the British language at present. It was used in the name of Prydæn among his Cimbri of Brigantia, in the days of Llomarch Hen [1]; and in the name of Prudain

[1] Lhuyd, p. 219.

among his Cimbri of Wales, in the earlier days of Pabo [1]. And it exists in the Welsh Prydhain and the Cornish Prydein, the Welsh Brython and Brythoneg, and the Armorican Brezon and Brezonnec, to the present period. The new name of Britain, therefore, extended itself to Mr. Macpherson's Gael, both in Caledonia and in Ireland, as it remains in the common language of both to the present day. And the name of Britain must, for that reason, not have been imposed upon the island, by any body of colonists that were distinct from, and even in hostility with, the Gael. It must have been affixed from some principle of discrimination that equally affected all, and must have been adopted by all as the one national note of distinction. And it accordingly appears to have been common to every division of the islanders. Given and assumed at the first migration of colonists into Albion, as the natural signature of their sequestration from their brethren in Gaul; it was never the denomination either imposed or retained exclusively by a part, but was at once coæval with the plantation of the island, and commensurate with the colonies of the islanders.

[1] Mona, p. 158, second Edit.

II.

CONCERNING MR. MACPHERSON's FIRST POPULATION OF IRELAND BY THE CALEDONIANS.

PAG. 41. "The Cimbri and Belgæ, after "they were comprehended within the pale "of the Roman dominions, were seen diſtinctly; "but the more ancient inhabitants of the iſland, "the Gael, appeared only tranſiently, when, in "an hoſtile manner, they advanced to the fron- "tiers of the province. The arms of the empire "penetrated, at different periods, into the heart "of the country beyond the Scottiſh Friths; "but as theſe expeditions were not attended "with abſolute conqueſt, and a conſequent ſet- "tlement of colonies, the Romans made little "inquiry concerning the origin and hiſtory of "the natives of the northern diviſion of Bri- "tain."

I do not love to ſuppoſe contradictions in an author of Mr. Macpherſon's merit, and eſpecially

within

within the compafs only of a few lines. It feems
fo unlikely, that I am rather inclined to difbe-
lieve the fuggeftions of my own judgement.
And yet I have already obferved fuch an haftinefs in the compofition of the prefent work,
and fome contradictions which, feemingly at
leaft, are fo grofs, that I cannot give up my
feelings to an affectation of fairnefs, and facri-
fice precifion to politenefs.—We are here firft
told, that the Gael appeared only tranfiently to
the Romans, when in an hoftile manner they
advanced to the frontiers of the Roman province.
And yet immediately afterwards we are told,
that the Romans penetrated at different periods
into the heart of their country. Is not this contradictory? And is not the whole paffage in direct oppofition to another in p. 22, 23? We are
here affured, that the Cimbri and Belgæ were,
and that the Gael were not, feen diftinctly by
the Romans. But there we find, that " the in-
" formation of the Romans accompanied the
" progrefs of their arms; new communities rofe
" gradually before them as they advanced into
" the heart of the ifland; till *the whole body*
" of its inhabitants came forward *diftinctly* to
" view, when Agricola carried the Roman eagles
" to the mountains of Caledonia."

The great pofition in this extract is, that the
Caledonians were but little known to the Romans, becaufe they were never comprehended
within

within the pale of the Roman empire. The fact is not true. And the reasoning is not just.

Many nations were well-known to the Romans, that were never comprehended within the pale of their empire. Ireland is a remarkable instance of this, where we have all the tribes recited, all the towns enumerated, and all the headlands and rivers specified, equally as in the provinces of Britain. As the Roman empire extended itself upon every side, the Roman geographers and historians enlarged the circle of their observations, gained an acquaintance with all the nations that bordered upon their frontiers, and carried their researches where the arms of their countrymen never penetrated. And Mr. Macpherson in another place, and to serve another purpose, not only allows but contends for it. "It is morally impossible," says he in p. 190, "that a migration sufficient to people Caledonia "and *Ireland*, could have happened, without "falling within the knowledge of the writers of "Rome, who *certainly extended their enquiries to* "*the transactions of the wild nations on the fron-* "*tiers of the empire.*"

But the fact is not true, that the Caledonians were unknown to the Romans, because they were never comprehended within the empire. Since some of them were comprehended, those must have been fully known, as fully as the Cimbri

and

and the Belgæ. Since several of them were, several must have been known as fully. As many were reduced by the Romans, the Romans must have been conversant with a considerable part of Caledonia. And as the greater part of the tribes submitted to their power, the greater part of the country must have been open to their observations. That this was actually the case, may be easily shewn. The Gael or Caledonians are placed by Mr. Macpherson, before, in the large division of the island which runs from the Tweed to the Orkneys. "The Cimbri," he says in p. 32, "— possessed — the country — from the "Humber to the Tweed. The Gael, under the "general name of Caledonians, inhabited the "rest of the island to the extremity of the North." Now this region comprehended no less than twenty-one tribes [1]. And no fewer than eleven of these had been actually subdued by the Romans, and brought within the pale of their empire, being formed into the province of Valentia to the South of the Friths, and of Vespasiana to the North of them [2]. Vespasiana continued a province from the year 140 to 170 [3]. And Valentia remained one, from the days of Agricola to the late period of the Roman departure [4]. The

---

[1] History of Manchester, p. 63, and 409—411.
[2] Ibid.   [3] History of Manchester, p. 419.
[4] History of Manchester, p. 453—458.

Gael

Gael therefore, that refided to the South of the Friths, not only appeared to the Romans by advancing frequently to the frontiers of the provinces, but were all engaged with the Romans, were all fubdued by them, and were all reduced into a province. They did not merely appear tranfiently and occafionally to them, but were actually invaded, actually conquered, and actually retained in fubjection for no lefs than three centuries and a half. They were equally comprehended within the circle of the Roman empire as the Cimbri and the Belgæ, were equally comprehended with both in the firft century, and equally continued in it with both to the middle of the fifth. And, as to the Gael that lay to the North of the Friths, even many of thefe, no lefs than fix whole tribes, were entirely fubdued by the Romans; the Horeftii, the Vecturiones, the Taixali, the Vacomagi, the Damnii Albani, and the Attacotti [1]: and the Romans profecuted their conquefts, over the mountains of Athol and Badenoch, as far as Invernefs. No colonies indeed were fettled there, as none alfo were fettled in Valentia. Colonies were not the neceffary confequence of abfolute conqueft. Stations only were. And numerous ftations were planted to the North of the Friths, as Alauna, Lindum, and

[1] Hiftory of Manchefter, p. 410.

Victoria,

Victoria, among the Horeftii; Orrea, Ad Hiernam, Ad Tavum, Ad Eficam, and Ad Tinam, among the Vecturiones; and others in Strathern, Menteith, Badenoch, Braidalbin, Athol, and Invernefs[1]. The Romans therefore, who had penetrated into the center of the Highlands, who fettled in all the conquered regions from the Friths to Invernefs, and who even made an aftronomical obfervation, which is ftill preferved, at the town of Invernefs[2], could not be ignorant of the countries in which they refided, could not be uninformed concerning the region which immediately bordered upon them, and muft have been fufficiently converfant with all Caledonia. Intimately acquainted, as they were, with the interiors of an ifland which they had never vifited at all, Ireland; they muft have been much better acquainted with the interiors of Caledonia, in the heart of which they were encamped for thirty years together, and where their fcholars appear to have been particularly obfervant.

Mr. Macpherfon's remark therefore, that his Caledonians were little known to the Romans, becaufe they appeared only tranfiently upon the frontiers of their empire, or becaufe they were never abfolutely reduced by their armies, appears to be equally unjuft in the reafoning and falfe in

[1] Hiftory of Manchefter, p. 409, 410.
[2] Hiftory of Manchefter, p. 56.

the fact. The Romans were well acquainted with Ireland, though they never visited it. The Romans actually reduced three fourths of Mr. Macpherson's Caledonians. The Romans must have been well acquainted with a people, with whom, as friends or as enemies, they had a continual and uninterrupted intercourse of nearly four centuries. And the Romans have actually left us a very particular account of all the tribes of Caledonia, in Ptolemy and in Richard.

P. 41, 42. "Julius Agricola, who, for the "first time, displayed the Roman eagles beyond "the Friths, was not more successful in the field "than he was happy in an historian to transmit "his actions with lustre to posterity. But even "the distinct and intelligent Tacitus gives but a "very imperfect idea of those enemies, by the "defeat of whom his father-in-law acquired so "much reputation. We learn from him indeed "that the Caledonians were the most antient in- "habitants of Britain."

Here the author evidently fixes the Caledonians beyond the Friths. And yet, as I have shewed in the last article, he brings them in p. 32. down as low as the Tweed. How inaccurate!—And here is also another great inaccuracy. From Tacitus we learn, if we may ascribe the speech of Galgacus to him, not that the Caledonians were the moſt antient inhabitants of Britain, but that they were the moſt honourable, nobiliſſimi totius Britanniæ. And flouriſhes like that, in ſuch addreſſes as Galgacus's, it is idle to adduce for an hiſtorical authority.

P. 42—44. "This is the ſum of what the Romans have related concerning the Caledonians for near two centuries after they were firſt mentioned: to their origin and internal hiſtory they were equally ſtrangers. — Had the Romans eſtabliſhed themſelves in Caledonia, we might indeed have known more of the antient inhabitants of that country —. The firſt domeſtic writers of the hiſtory of North Britain were too ignorant, as well as too modern, to form any probable ſyſtem concerning the origin of their nation."

I have already ſhewn, that the Romans did eſtabliſh themſelves in Caledonia, and that they reduced one half even of the genuine Caledonians, the Britons to the North of the Friths. And as to the ignorance of the Romans, concerning the interior hiſtory and origin of the Caledonians before their invaſion, they were alſo ignorant of the interior hiſtory and origin of the Britons in general. Whence the Britons were derived, when they came into the island, and how they gradually diffused their spreading numbers to the farthest promontories of Caledonia, was all equally unknown to them.

P. 47, 48. " In proportion as the Cimbri advanced towards the North, the Gael, being circumscribed within narrower limits, were forced to transmigrate into the islands which crowd the Northern and Western coasts of Scotland. It is in this period, perhaps, we ought to place the first great migration of the British Gael into Ireland; that kingdom being much nearer to the promontory of Galloway and Cantyre, than many of the Scottish isles are to the continent of North Britain. This vicinity of Ireland had probably drawn partial emigrations from Caledonia before the arrival of the Cimbri in Britain; but when these interlopers pressed upon the Gael from the South, it is reasonable to conclude that numerous colonies passed over into an island so near, and so much superior to their original country in climate and fertility."

I have already demonstrated, that no colony of the Cimbri, as distinct and different from the
Gael

Gael, ever landed in the island. And, consequently, all the transactions attributed to them must be absolutely false. This series of suppositions therefore is a chain of errors. As the Cimbri never advanced towards the North, the Gael could not have been circumscribed within narrower limits, or forced to transmigrate into the western isles of Scotland. As no such interlopers ever pressed upon the Gael, no colonies of them, either small or numerous, could have been induced by it to pass over into Ireland.

But I am obliged here to remark again the author's apparent inconsistency, with regard to the position of his Gael. In p. 32 they are ranged from the banks of the Tweed to the northern extremity of the island. In p. 41—44 they are ranged only to the North of the Friths. Here, in p. 47, they are brought down as low as Galloway again. And in p. 48 they are once more carried back to the Friths. It is there said, that, when the Belgæ " drove the Cimbri beyond " the Severne and Humber, the Gael of the " North, reduced within limits still more cir- " cumscribed by the pressure of the Cimbri, sent " fresh colonies into Ireland, while *the Scottish* " *Friths became a natural and strong boundary to-* " *wards the South to those Gael who remained in* " *Britain.*" And yet at this very period, even when the Cimbri inhabited betwixt the Humber and the Tweed, the Gael are said before to have

reached from the Tweed to the North. "The
"Cimbri,— retiring from the preffure of thefe
"new invaders [the Belgæ], poffeffed the coun-
"try — from the Humber to the Tweed. The
"Gael, under the general name of Caledonians,
"inhabited the reft of the ifland to the extremity
"of the North [1]." So unfettled is the author in
his notions concerning the Britifh topography of
the ifland, and fo varying and contradictory in his
reprefentations of it.

P. 48. "The inhabitants of the maritime re-
"gions of Gaul croffing, in an after age [after
"the Cimbri], the Britifh channel (*maritima pars*
"*Britanniæ ab iis*, qui prædæ ac belli inferendi
"causâ, ex Belgis tranfierant : . . . et bello il-
"lato ibi remanferunt, atque agros colere coepe-
"runt. Cæfar de Bell. Gall. lib. v.), eftablifhed
"themfelves on that part of our ifland which lies
"neareft to the continent ; and, moving gradu-
"ally towards the North, drove the Cimbri be-
"yond the Severn and Humber."

I have brought this paffage out to view, merely
to fhew one among many inftances of Mr. Macpherfon's ftrange behaviour towards his quotations. He afferts the Belgæ to have carried their
poffeffions up to the Humber. And he afferts

[1] P. 32.

it upon the ftrength of a quotation, of which he has italicifed the principal words; when that very quotation, and thofe very words, do in the fulleft manner confine the Belgæ to the fouthern fhore. This is furely a very extraordinary fpecimen of inattention and inaccuracy.

P. 48, 49. "It was, perhaps, after the Bel-
"gic invafion of the Southern Britain, that
"the Gael of the Northern divifion formed
"themfelves into a regular community, to repel
"the incroachment of the Cimbri upon their
"territories. To the country which they them-
"felves poffeffed they gave the name of CAEL-
"DOCH, which is the only appellation the
"Scots, who fpeak the Galic language, know
"for their own divifion of Britain. CAEL-
"DOCH is a compound made up of Gael or
"Caël, the firft colony of the antient Gauls
"who tranfmigrated into Britain, and DOCH,
"a diftrict or divifion of a country. The Ro-
"mans, by tranfpofing the letter L in Caël,
"and by foftening into a Latin termination the
"*ch* of DOCH, formed the well-known name
"of Caledonia. Obvious as this Etymon of
"Caledonia appears, it was but very lately dif-
"covered. (This Etymon firft occurred to the
"author of this Effay, and he communicated

" it to Dr. Macpherson, who adopted it from
" a conviction of its juſtneſs). Thoſe who
" treated of the antiquities of North Britain
" were utter ſtrangers to that only name by which
" the Scots diſtinguiſhed the corner of Britain
" which their Anceſtors poſſeſſed from the re-
" moteſt antiquity. From an ignorance, ſo un-
" pardonable in antiquaries, proceeded that er-
" roneous ſyſtem, &c. '."

I have made this large extract, to exhibit the whole argument in all its force, and, I may add, in all its oſtentation too. And I ſhall now endeavour to ſhew the reaſonings to be as feeble and the etymons as injudicious, even in this triumphant paſſage, as in any that I have diſſected before.

The aſſertions in this paragraph are theſe, That the Caledonians perhaps firſt formed themſelves into one community, to repel the incroachments of the Cimbri; That a proof of this incorporation remains in the word Caeldoch, which ſignifies the Diſtrict of the Gael; and, That this word is the Latin Caledonia. Each ſhall be conſidered diſtinctly.

The incroachments of the Cimbri muſt be as imaginary, as the reſt of their hiſtory. And any aſſociation of the Caledonians, to repel them,

---

¹ This Etymon is in Dr. Macpherſon, p. 27. and 100.— And he makes the ſame uſe of the name of Gael in p. 97, 98, and of Caeldoch in p. 100.

muſt

must be equally visionary with both. The first time that the Caledonians embodied into one empire, was assuredly the period which is assigned for it in the History of Manchester [1]. The Romans under Agricola were certainly the first common enemy, which had hitherto attacked them. Nothing but such an attack could have induced them to form themselves into one monarchy. And into one monarchy they actually first formed themselves at that period. *Æstate quâ sextum officii annum inchoabat* [Agricola], *amplas civitates trans Bodotriam sitas, quia motus univerfarum ultra gentium,* et *infesta hostili exercitu itinera, timebantur, prius classe exploravit* [2]. In the commencement of the 6th year of Agricola's Proconsulate therefore, or in the spring of the year 83, the Caledonians were not yet associated into one community. Agricola only apprehended that they would speedily associate, as the danger became more imminent to all. And in this and the year following they actually combined. *Ad manus et arma conversi Caledoniam incolentes populi ;—nihil remittere, quo minus juventutem armarent, conjuges ac liberos in loca tuta transferrent, coetibus ac sacrificiis conspirationem civitatum sancirent ; tandem*--docti *commune periculum concordiâ propulsandum* [3]. The Caledonians therefore did

[1] P. 414. [2] Agric. V. c. 25. [3] C. 25, 27, and 29.

not model their tribes into one community, in consequence of the Cimbric incroachments upon them. There were no such incroachments made. And there were no Cimbri, or German Celtæ, to make them. The Caledonians actually embodied together long after the æra assigned for it by Mr. Macpherson, when Agricola threatened the reduction of all their tribes.

Nor is the name of Caeldoch, now used by the Highlanders to signify their country, any proof of such an association. It is no proof of any association at all. And the etymon, which is here displayed with such an air of consequence, and with such a reflection upon the ignorance of others, is obviously unjust in itself. This will easily appear.—I have previously shewn Gathel to be pronounced similarly to Gael by the Irish and Highlanders. And Gathel is also changed, as I have equally remarked, into Galath, Galat, Galt, and Celt. It is also changed into Gaellt, Gallt, Gaeld, and Gald[1]. This we see directly exemplified in the Gael of the continent and of the island being universally denominated Galatæ and Celtæ by the Græcians, Gallt and

[1] See Buchanan, p. 34, 35. and p. 61. V. I. Ruddiman, who informs us, that the Scotch use the word Gald for a Gaul. And see also Gauld-i and Gaelti, and even Gaeltach, in Dr. Macpherson, p. 98, 99. — From the word Gald is derived the name for Galgacus in the Scotch Romances, Galdus. — And see Irwin's Hist. Scot. Nomen-clatura Latino-vernacula, 1682, p. 83.

Gallta by the Irish, and Gaelt, Gallt, and Gald by the Highlanders. And the relative adjective of this word is the very name, which Mr. Macpherson has so ingeniously distorted here. Gael and Cael lengthening into Gal-ek and Cael-ich, Gallt must be formed into Gallt-ach, and Gaeld into Gaeld-ach. And we actually have Gallt-ach in the Irish language, the appellation for a Gaul at present. Gaeld-och and Gallt-ach therefore are one and the same word, the relative adjectives of the same national appellation, Gaeld and Gallt; and, in the spirit of all other relative adjectives, refer equally to an individual, the language, or the country, of France and Scotland. Thus easily is the mighty spell dissolved, which held both Dr. and Mr. Macpherson in absolute bondage. And thus readily is the great fabrick destroyed, which was raised by the magic hand of error, equally slight in its structure, and momentary in its continuance.

That Caeldoch is the very same word with Caledonia, is another of Mr. Macpherson's positions. But it is equally a mistake. And I hope convincingly to prove it. I shall lay before the reader what I have said upon this subject in the History of Manchester, and I shall make some additions to it.—I have previously shewn the words Gathel, Gael, Galat, Galt, Gaeld, and Celt, to be all one and the same appellation. And though Mr. Macpherson

Macpherſon in p. 10 ſeems inclined to derive one of them, Gaul, from the Celtic Geal, Fair, a deſignation evidently too effeminate for the bold and ferocious Celtæ ; they all ſignify a Woodlander. Geil-t, Guylh-t, and Guel-z, among the Iriſh, the Welſh, and the Armoricans, import a Man of the Kelli, Guylh, or Gnel, a Wood ; all of them the evident remains of the antient and obſolete Guid*h*il or Gue*th*el a Wood. And ſeveral woods in Wales are actually denominated Cottel to this day¹. Coil, the ſame with the Cottel, the Guylh, and the Kelli, of the Welſh, and anſwering to Gathel, Gael, and Cael, is the cuſtomary term for a Wood among the Iriſh and Highlanders at preſent. And Gulad occurs in Gulad-ædh, the Welſh for a Woodlander ; Kelyd appears in Kelydhon, the Britiſh for Woods ; and Gelht remains undiſguiſed in the Welſh language at preſent ; all correſponding to Galat, Galt, Gaeld, and Celt, and all ſignifying with them a Wood. The celebrated appellations therefore of Gathel-i, Galat-æ, Calet-es, An-Calit-es, and Celtæ, all import a Wood only. And bearing the Celtic prefix before them, which is uſed in the antient Hiſtory of Ireland, as Fir-Bolg and Fir-Damnon, and which is equally uſed in this very appellation by the Iriſh of the preſent moment, as Gallta or Fear-Gallta ; the denomina-

¹ Mr. Lhuyd in Nº. 2. Appendix to Nicholſon's Scottiſh Hiſt. Library.

tions

tions of Fir-Galat, Fir-Galt, Fir-Gaeld, and Fir-Celt muſt have ſignified merely the Man of the Wood. But, in two national denominations of the very ſame origin, the termination is a little different, becauſe the words are in the plural number, or ſtand as the relative adjective. Kelyd or Caled lengthens into Kelyd-on or Caled-on, Woods; and Gallt or Gaeld is formed into Gallt-ach or Gaeld-och, Woodland-iſh. Thus Caledon became the antient appellation for all the extenſive Foreſts of the Gatheli and the Galli in the provinces of Britain; from the Foreſt of Anderida in Kent, Suſſex, and ſeveral other counties, into which, under the name of the Caledonian Woods, Florus ſays that Cæſar purſued the Britons; to the Foreſt of the Coritani in Lincolnſhire and ſome adjoining counties, to which, under the ſame denomination of the Caledonian Wood, Pliny ſays that the Roman arms had been carried in his time; and to the well-known Caledonian Foreſt of Scotland [1]. Thus Fir-Caledon, or Caledones, and the equivalent Gaeld-och, became equally the antient and preſent appellations for the Gathel and the Gael of the Highlands. And thus Caledonius became occaſionally among the Romans a denomination equivalent to Britannicus, and was applied equally

---

[1] Florus, L. iii. c. 10. Caledonias ſecutus in ſilvas; Pliny, L. iv. c. 16; and Hiſtory of Mancheſter, p 415, and 337.

with

with it to all the Gathel and Gael in the ifland [1].— The word Caeldoch therefore is very different from the word Caledonia. Derived from the fame root, and carrying the fame power, they are very different branches. The one is a relative adjective; the other is a Noun Subftantive. The one is derived from Gaeld in the fingular; the other is deduced from Caledon in the plural. And the one is the fame word with Celticus, and the other with Galatarum.

I have been thus particular upon the fubject, becaufe it is of fome confequence in itfelf, and Mr. Macpherfon introduces it with fuch a fond regard. And I think that I have fully demonftrated Mr. Macpherfon's reafonings and etymons to be advanced, equally in oppofition to the voice of hiftory, and to the principles of the Celtic language.

P. 49, 50.— " Concerning the internal
" ftate of Caledonia, and the divifion of its inha-
" bitants into various tribes in a very early

---

[1] Hiftory of Manchefter, p. 439, 440.— And there is an additional proof of it, that has never been noticed, in thefe lines of Lucan, in which the Caledonians are firft mentioned in hiftory, and which call the Britons about Richborough Caledonians:

Aut vaga cum Tethys Rutupinaque littora fervent,
Unda Caledonios fallit turbata Britannos.

" period,

"period, we can find nothing certain. The
" account given by Ptolemy of the Epidii, Ca-
" rini, Cantæ, Logæ, and other nations, is little
" to be regarded. Tacitus paffed over thofe
" petty communities in filence; and in the period
" between the expedition of Julius Agricola,
" and the reign of Marcus Aurelius, under
" whom the Egyptian geographer flourifhed,
" the Romans had no opportunity of being
" acquainted with the domeftic arrangements of
" the Caledonians."

In this paffage Mr. Macpherfon rejects Ptolemy's account of the internal ftate of Caledonia, and of its divifion into various tribes, becaufe Tacitus paffes over thefe communities in filence; and becaufe, from the days of Tacitus to the time of Ptolemy, the Romans had no opportunity of knowing the domeftic arrangements of the Caledonians. The former is furely a very trifling reafon. And the latter is certainly a falfe fact.

The filence of Tacitus, concerning the tribes of Caledonia, is no proof that he was not acquainted with the divifions. He has not even fpecified any of the tribes, that Agricola conquered from the Dee to the Friths. And yet Mr. Macpherfon will not deny the partition of the country into tribes, He actually acknowledges it in this very page and in p. 51, fpeaking
of

of the Selgovæ, the Gadeni, the Damnii, the Novantes, and the Ottadini, five of thofe tribes, and whom he knows only from Ptolemy. In p. 82 alfo he exprefsly quotes the authority of Ptolemy for the Brigantes, the Velaborii, the Cauci, and the Menapii, in Ireland; though the Romans never had any opportunity at all, in Mr. Macpherfon's acceptation of the word, to know the interior divifion of the country. And in p. 63 he argues, that even the *manners* of the Irifh muft have been perfectly known to the Romans, though here he denies them to have known even the names and pofitions of the Caledonian tribes, and though he allows the Romans to have had continual wars with the one, and none at all with the other. So inconfiftent is Mr. Macpherfon with himfelf! So much does he warp with the variations and bearings of his favourite hypothefis!

The defign of Tacitus and Ptolemy was very different. That was compofing an hiftorical narration of national tranfactions; this was writing a geographical account of the nations. The one was obliged to detail to us the names, the fites, and the towns, of the various tribes that crouded the face of the ifland. But the other was required only to give us general defcriptions and general appellations, fuch notices only as were juft fufficient to lend propriety and meaning to the actions, and to exhibit the actors and their principles

principles in a strong point of view. Tacitus therefore does not enumerate the tribes of Caledonia; and Ptolemy does. Tacitus does not specify any particular nations; but he speaks expressly of them in general. And Mr. Macpherson's argument again fails. Amplas civitates trans Bodotriam sitas; motus universarum ultra gentium; Caledoniam incolentes populi; conspirationem civitatum; and, omnium civitatum vires [1]. From the officers of Agricola, therefore, might the Romans have derived that knowledge of the domestic arrangements of the Caledonians, which Ptolemy has presented to us. And, even additional to this source of intelligence, Ptolemy had the finest opportunity that ever a geographer had, of knowing the internal disposition of Caledonia compleatly, from the remarkable war of which Mr. Macpherson appears to be totally unapprized, the invasion of Caledonia by Lollius Urbicus about the year 140, and the reduction of half of it beneath the dominion of the Romans [2]. And Ptolemy, as I have previously remarked, has actually given us an astronomical observation, which was made at Inverness, and which could have been made only in consequence of that reduction.

---

[1] Agric. V. 25, 27, and 30.
[2] See History of Manchester, p. 55, 56, and 418, 419.

P. 50.

P. 50. "Though the Scottish Friths are generally allowed to have been the boundaries of Caledonia towards the South, it is more than probable that those tribes who possessed the country between the walls were principally descended from the antient Gael. The names of the Selgovæ and Gadeni, two petty communities on the northern banks of the Solway and Tweed, seem to strengthen this supposition. They carry in their signification a proof that the tribes who bore them were in a state of hostility with their neighbours the Ottadini and Brigantes, which furnishes a presumption that they derived their origin from a different quarter. (Selgovæ is plainly Selgovich latinized. Selgovich literally signifies *Hunters*, in a metaphorical sense *Plunderers* —. Gadeni is plainly from *Gadechin*, Robbers; a name which arose from the same love of depredation with their friends and neighbours the Selgovæ [1].)."

I have more than once remarked already the strange doubling of the present dissertation, in sometimes bringing down the Gael or Caledonians to the banks of the Tweed, and in sometimes carrying them up to the North of the

[1] The same etymons of Selgovæ and Gadeni are given by Dr. Macpherson in p. 112.

Friths. And the fame fpirit occurs here again. We have before been informed pofitively and without hefitation, that " the Gael, under the " general name of Caledonians, inhabited from " the Tweed to the extremity of the North." But we are here informed, that their inhabiting from the Tweed to the Friths is only " more " than probable," that Mr. Macpherfon " fup- " pofes it," and that there is " a prefumption " for it. The certainty in p. 32 is all dwindled away in p. 50. And as the reader proceeds in the work, and naturally expects a clearer light and ftronger convictions, he finds his author himfelf faultering in his ftyle, and becoming more dubious of his own pofitions.

The Caledonians were brought down at firft to the Solway and the Tweed, and are occafionally brought down at prefent, merely becaufe of the name of Galloway there; as the name of Cumberland occafioned the Cimbri, before, to be planted betwixt the Humber and the Tweed. And the Caledonians were carried at firft, and are occafionally carried at prefent, to the North of the Friths, becaufe hiftory exprefsly places them to the North. The two ftrong and active principles, thus unwarily blended together, are continually ftruggling for fuperiority, and fometimes the one colour and fometimes the other predominates.—But the reafon here adduced, for the refidence of the Caledonians betwixt the

K   Walls,

Walls, is even feebler and more trifling than the secret reason before. The names of Selgovæ and Gadeni, it is said, *prove* the tribes to have been in a state of hostility with the Cimbric Ottadini and Brigantes. But why not with the Caledonians? There is no more reason for that than this. And then the argument is not only repelled, but actually changes sides, and militates directly against its master.

But I am tired with pursuing such impertinencies. And yet others present themselves before us. Mr. Macpherson is greatly mistaken both in his Geography and Etymology.—Selgovæ, he says, signifies Hunters, and metaphorically Robbers. But the metaphor is such as contradicts every idea of propriety. And it is such peculiarly, as no nation and age of Hunters could ever have tolerated. Selgovæ appears from Ptolemy to be Elgovæ with a Prefix, being written by him Selgovæ in one place and Elgovæ in another. And the root of the name is therefore to be sought in Elgovæ, and is probably this. The æstuary formed by the river Eden was pretty certainly denominated S, Alga, Av, or The Noble Water, as Ireland has been sometimes denominated Inis Alga in Irish, and as a Peninsula on the banks of the Lossie in Scotland, seems to have been called Elgin formerly [1].

[1] So another peninsula, formed by the streams of the

The name remains to this day in its prefent appellation of the SOLWAY Frith, as the antient name of Conovius continues in that of the Conway at prefent. And the tribe, that inhabited along the whole extended line of the æftuary, was naturally denominated Fir-Elgovæ or Fir-Selgovæ, Men, or the Men, of the Great Water.— Gadeni is alfo interpreted Robbers, and to be the fame word with the Irifh Gadechin, Robbers. The real word in Irifh, I believe, is not Gadechin, but Gaduighe a thief, and Gaduighen Thieves. And Gadeni plainly comes from Gadh or Cath a Fight, as Crutheni is derived from Cruth; and, like Camulo-genus, the name of a Gallic Hero in Cæfar [1], fignifies the Men of the Battle, or the Warriours. And the Gadeni are therefore denominated the Cadeni, in a Roman-Britifh infcription difcovered in the North [2].—Nor were the Gadeni bounded merely by the northern bank of the Tweed, or the Ottadini by the fouthern, as Mr. Macpherfon places them. The Gadeni ranged from the Wall to the North of Lanerk. And the Ottadini, whom the Author fuppofes to lie all to the South of the Tweed, extended beyond it to the Friths [3]. Mr. Macpherfon's great divifion of

Loffie and the Spey, was called Inis, an ifland, having the two villages of Innes and Ince in it to this day.

[1] Cæfar, p. 164. [2] Horfeley, Nº. 80. Northumberland.
[3] Hiftory of Manchefter, p. 63.

the North to the Cimbri and the Gael is therefore entirely overturned, as his great partition of the South to the Cimbri and the Belgæ was overturned before. Those whom he denominates Cimbri and oppofes to the Gael, the Cimbric Ottadini of p. 51, lived only in a fmall part of the country which he has affigned to the Cimbri, and poffeffed alfo a large portion of that region which he has allotted to the Gael. But this is not all. The whole " country between the " Walls" Mr. Macpherfon here refigns up to the Gael, as the Selgovæ, the Gadeni, and others; whom he engages in hoftility with, and therefore fuppofes to be of a different origin from, the Ottadini immediately to the South of the nearer Wall. But the whole body of the Ottadinian dominions, except a very fmall flip of land along the fouthern edge of Northumberland, was actually to the North of the nearer Wall'. Mr. Macpherfon cedes all " the country betwixt " the Walls" to his Gael, and therefore brings them down to the northern banks of the Solway and Tweed. But he is not aware, that the nearer Wall did not run from the Solway to the Tweed. It began on the Solway: but it ended on the Tyne.

Thus have I laid open the numerous miftakes in this remarkable paffage. I have fhewn the

[1] Ibid.

reafonings,

reasonings, I think, to be at once arbitrary in their principles, and frivolous in their conclusions. And I have demonstrated the Geography of the island, I think, to be at once false and contradictory.

P. 51. " As that tract of country which is
" comprehended between the Tweed and Solway,
" and the Scottish Friths, was more exposed to
" invasion than Caledonia, we may conclude
" that the Gael who possessed it were, in some
" degree, mixed with the Cimbric Ottadini and
" Brigantes, even before the invasions of the
" Romans pressed those tribes towards the North.
" It was from this unavoidable mixture that the
" Selgovæ, Gadeni, Damnii, and Novantes, were,
" in an after-age, distinguished by the name of
" Mæatæ, which signifies a people descended
" from a double origin, as well as the inhabitants
" of a controverted country. (Moi-atta, or Moi-
" atich, the inhabitants of the Plains: Mæan-
" atta, the possessors of the Middle country[1]:
" Moai-atta, a mixed people)."

The errors in this part of the Dissertation seem to rise before us every step that we take, and are perpetually stopping us in our progress. This passage immediately follows the former.

[1] These two etymons are given by Dr. Macpherson, p. 23.

The former was the laſt of four or five ſucceſſive Extracts. And this is as pregnant with miſtakes as any of them.

If the mixture of Mr. Macpherſon's Ottadini and Brigantes with his Gael betwixt the Walls, was, as Mr. Macpherſon alledges, *unavoidable*, becauſe the country betwixt the Walls was the frontier of Caledonia; the ſame mixture muſt have been equally unavoidable, on the frontiers of the Belgæ and the Cimbri in Wales and in Maxima. The region betwixt the Solway, the Tweed, and the Friths, is not more " expoſed " to invaſion," than the land behind the Severne and the Dee, or the tract betwixt the Humber, the Merſey, the Tweed, and the Eden. And ſince the country to the South of the Solway and the Tweed muſt have been equally expoſed to invaſion, as the country to the North of them, the barriers of both being exactly the ſame; the ſame *unavoidable* mixture muſt have equally enſued in Northumberland as in the Lothians &c., and in Cumberland as in Anandale &c. The reaſoning therefore is not only inaccurate, but carries an edge with it, that, " like " an ill-ſheathed knife, will cut its maſter[1]."

The facts alſo and the etymons are both equally untrue.—I have previouſly ſhewn the Ottadini not to have been Cimbric, even upon Mr. Mac-

---

[1] Shakeſpear.

pherſon's

pherson's own argument. And the invasion of the Romans pressed no tribes towards the North. All appear to have possessed exactly the same divisions of the country before the Romans came, as they enjoyed afterwards. And this is particularly the case with respect to the Brigantes. They had reduced the Selgovæ before [1]. But the Gadeni, the Novantes, and the Damnii were totally unmixed either with Ottadini or Brigantes. And this *unavoidable* mixture is false in fact.—The name of Mæatæ, also, belonged not to any tribes betwixt the Walls, but to some that lay to the North of the more northerly Wall. This indeed has been considerably doubted. But it may be easily proved. In the History of Manchester I have already shewn, to the fullest conviction, I believe, of every mind, that the Romans retained the province betwixt the Walls regularly in their own possession, from the period of its first conquest to the æra of their departure from the island [2]. And the expedition of the Emperor Severus was, therefore, against the Britons that lay to the North of Antoninus's Vallum. The Mæatæ then whom he reduced, who afterwards revolted, and to whom Caracalla resigned up all the conquests of his Father, must have been some tribes to the North of that

[1] History of Manchester, p. 104.
[2] History of Manchester, p. 453. 458.

Vallum.—And thus wrong in the position of the Mæatæ, Mr. Macpherson is sure to be wrong in his explanation of their name. And it is neither just in its own nature, nor right in its application to them. It is not just, because in the Text it equally gives two, and, still more strangely, in the Note equally annexes three, very different imports to the word; the inhabitants of the Plains; the possessors of a middle country, or (as to humour his Hypothesis, he contradictorily calls it in the Text) a controverted one; and a mixed people. All three were certainly not meant by the name. And, of the two mentioned in the Text, neither was meant at all. This is obvious from the impropriety of deducing Mæatæ from Moai-atich, and the greater impropriety of deducing it from Mæan-atich. And even the derivation of it from Moi-atich, which is the best of them all, and had been previously adopted in the History of Manchester[1], appears to me now to be harsh and forced. How Mr. Macpherson could be induced to give this interpretation in the Note, I cannot conceive; as it plainly stands in direct opposition to the reasonings and etymons in the Text. And the real etymology of the name, I believe, is this. Mag, a Plain, must have been equally pronounced May and Mæ originally, as

[1] P. 415.

it naturally would be, and as it is now written Mæs in Welſh and Moi in Iriſh. And the inhabitants of the lower lands of Caledonia, which lie immediately to the North of Antoninus's Vallum, and along the line of the Eaſtern coaſt, would naturally be diſtinguiſhed from the reſt of the Caledonians, the Mountaineers upon one ſide of them, by ſome topical and deſcriptive appellation. The Mountaineers are thus diſcriminated at preſent by the title of Albanech or Highlanders. And the others are to this day frequently denominated the Lowlanders. May or Mæ, a Plain, runs out into Mai-ed or Mæ-at in the plural. And as we have ſeen Fir-Gallt and Fir-Caledon above, and as the Carnabii and Cantii muſt have been originally Fir-Cant and Fir-Carnab, ſo Mæatæ muſt have been Fir-Mæ-at, and ſignifies the Men of the Plains.

I have dwelt the longer upon this paſſage, to lay open the inaccurate mode of reaſoning which is uſed by Mr. Macpherſon, the very bold manner in which he advances ſuppoſitions into certainty, and his ſtrange method of contradicting in the Notes what he aſſerts in the Text. The reaſoning here is peculiarly looſe and flimſy. The aſſertions are uncommonly ſtrong and arbitrary. And the contradiction of the Note to the Text is remarkably ſtriking.

P. 54.

P. 54. Our author, having in p. 52, 53 satisfactorily proved from the Greek and Roman writers, that the antient Irish were the descendants of the Britons, says thus — "The name of Gael, still "retained by the old Irish, sufficiently demon- "strates that they derive their blood from those "Gael or Gauls, who, in an after period, were "distinguished in Britain by the name of Cale- "donians. The wildest enthusiasts in Hibernian "antiquities never once asserted that the Cale- "donians, or their posterity the Picts, were of "Irish extract; yet nothing is better ascertained "than that the antient Britons of the South gave "to the Scots, the Picts, and the Irish, the com- "mon name of Gael; and consequently that they "very justly concluded that the three nations "derived their origin from the same source, the "antient Gael of the continent."

This *demonstration* is no argument at all. This will immediately appear. And a very slight examination will add one more proof to the many that we have had before, of Mr. Macpherson's unhappiness in the work of proving.

The Irish are said, by retaining the name of Gael, to prove themselves the descendants of the Caledonians. If the author here includes the country to the South of the Friths in the name of Caledonia, then he is once more in a state of hostility hoftility with some of his former pofitions and with all hiftory. If he does not, then the Irifh may be defcended from the Gael of Galloway. And, whether he does or not, his reafoning from the name of Gael is quite impertinent. The name is no evidence at all of the Caledonian defcent of the Irifh. It was not appropriated to the Caledonians either North or South of the Friths. It was, as I have previoufly fhewn, common to all the Britons, deduced with them from Gaul, and retained by them in all their iflands. And the Irifh might be equally *demonftrated* to be derived from the Gael of Wales, the Gael of Cornwall, or the Gael of Kent and Suffex.

The antient Britons of the South are alfo faid to have given the name of Gael to the Scots, the Picts, and the Irifh, and " confequently to have " very juftly concluded" them to be all one and the fame people. This conclufion, however, is not the antient Britons, but Mr. Macpherfon's. And it is not juft at all. Though the antient Britons of the South did call the Scots, the Picts, and the Irifh, by the common name of Gael, they did not mean to derive the firft and the laft from the second. They equally gave the name of Gael to themfelves, as I have fhewed before, to the tribes of Kent and Suffex, to the nations of Cornwall and Wales, and to all the Britons.

But the courfe of the author's reafoning here is very remarkable. He produces an argument

to

to prove, that the Irish were derived from the Caledonians. And at the close of it he concludes, that the Irish were derived — from the native Gauls. The name of Gael demonstrates the Irish to " derive their blood from *those Gael or Gauls,* " *who, in an after period, were distinguished by* " *the name of Caledonians.*" And the name of Gael proves the Scots, the Picts, and the Irish to have " derived their origin from the same source, " *the antient Gael of the continent.*" Vainly imagining, in opposition to the most obvious evidences, that the name of Gael in Britain was appropriated entirely to the Caledonians; and wildly supposing, in contradiction to the most express declarations of history, that the other tribes of Britain were German-Celtic; Mr. Macpherson goes on with a false association of ideas from the beginning to the close of his work, walking in one circle of errors, and plunging into absurdities and contradictions at every turn.

P. 54. a note. " Mr. O'Connor, who lately
" gave to the public some wild, incoherent
" tales, concerning the antient Irish, endea-
" vours to obviate the strength of the argu-
" ment, which rises against his system from the
" name of Gael, by disguising the word by the
" insertion of the intermediate letters, DH, as thus,
" *Gadhel.*

"*Gadhel.* The subterfuge avails nothing. DH
"are universally quiescent, or at most found
"like a Y, in every dialect of the Celtic lan-
"guage."

The argument deduced from Gael may be effectual against Mr. O'Connor's system, but, as I have already shewn, is of no force to establish Mr. Macpherson's. The indigenous appellation of Gael for the Irish serves strongly to evince them, what history demonstrates them to be, the descendants of the Britons. But it serves not in the least to point out the particular division of Britain, from which they were immediately derived.

Mr. Macpherson's intimate acquaintance with the Celtic language, was such an advantage over the body of our historical writers, that he might very justly, as he does in p. 5 and 38, plume himself considerably upon it. But I have previously remarked, that his knowledge of the Celtic appeared to be confined within the pale of a single dialect. And the present Extract confirms me in the opinion. Mr. Macpherson in p. 46 commends the author of the Critical Dissertations, for his "great knowledge *of all the* "*branches* of the Celtic language." The knowledge of both, however, seems to me to have been confined almost entirely to the Irish or Erse. It particularly seems so here. Mr. Macpherson could not otherwise have imagined, as he here asserts,

asserts, that DH are "universally quiescent, or "at most found like a Y, *in every dialect* of the "Celtic." And he re-asserts it in p. 148, saying that "Gaidhel, — as the DH are *invariably* "quiescent in Celtic words, is much the same "with Gael." This is very true concerning the Irish. But it is utterly untrue with regard to the Welsh particularly. This is a principal dialect of the Celtic. And the Welsh Guidhil, the same with the Irish Gaidhel, which Dr. Macpherson expressly asserts to be pronounced like it, Gael[1], is not pronounced like it at all, but actually and fully Guidhil. — We have also an instance of the same nature in p. 130. There the Welsh appellation for Ireland, Ywerdhon or Yverdhon, is said expressly to be "pronounced Yberon or "Yveron." And it is really pronounced, as it is written, Ywerdhon. — The author's and his friend's acquaintance with "every dialect of the "Celtic," did not extend to the Welsh. And his observation of the *invariable* quiescence of the DH in Celtic, and his friend's remark on the pronunciation of the word Guidhil, were both drawn, we see, from a view of the Irish only.

---

[1] See p. 97.

P. 54, 55.

P. 54, 55. "The British Gael, in an early age, "extending themselves to the very extremities "of the island, descried Ireland from the Mulls "of Galloway and Cantire, and crossing the nar- "row channel which separates the two countries, "became the progenitors of the Irish nation. In "proportion as fresh emigrants from the conti- "nent of Europe forced the antient Gael towards "the North in Britain, more colonies transmi- "grated into Ireland from the promontories which "we have so often mentioned."

The great historians of antiquity have claimed the privilege of being believed upon their own authority, and without any regular reference to the older chronicles. But the privilege is confined to them. Every modern historian that writes of a period preceding his own, of which he must know the incidents merely by tradition from others, is justly required to authenticate his accounts as he proceeds, and to produce sufficient vouchers for his facts. And the historical writer, that neglects this duty, must be content to see his work, perhaps, the favourite history of an hour, pleasing by its novelty, and engaging by its elegance, and then to have it resigned up to neglect and contempt for ever. — Here is the original inhabitation of Ireland by the Gael of Caledonia asserted, the place assigned from which

the

the original colony embarked, and the migration of additional colonies from the same place, in consequence of fresh invasions of Britain, affirmed; and all, without one article of authority, or one note of diffidence.

P. 55. " The Gael — became so numerous
" in that country [Ireland] before the arrival of
" the Belgæ in Britain, that the colonies which
" transmigrated from that nation into Ireland
" were, together with their language, manners,
" and customs, lost in the Gael; so that in one
" sense the Caledonians may be reckoned the
" sole progenitors of the old Irish. (The Fir-Bolg,
" so often mentioned in the traditions of the
" Irish, were Belgic colonies who transmigrated
" from Britain after the Belgæ had seized on the
" southern division of England. They are men-
" tioned very frequently under the name of Siol
" na m Bolga in the poems of Ossian."

The Gael are here said to have been " so nu-
" merous in Ireland before the arrival of the
" Belgæ in Britain," that, when the Belgæ came into Ireland, they were lost in the Gael. How very inconclusive! The Belgæ, when they came into Ireland, were lost in the Gael: and therefore the Gael, it is argued, must have been very

very numerous in Ireland, before the Belgæ arrived — in Britain. How ſtrangely inaccurate!

That the Belgæ were loſt in the Gael of Ireland, is a fact which is equally aſſerted and denied by Mr. Macpherſon in the preſent Extract. It is expreſsly aſſerted in the Text, and plainly denied in the Note. And I have ſhewn an inſtance of the ſame nature immediately before. The Belgæ, according to Mr. Macpherſon's own account in the Note, muſt have ſurvived for ages diſtinct from the Gael; or elſe no " traditions of " the Iriſh " could exiſt concerning them at preſent. The Belgæ, according to the ſame account in Mr. Macpherſon, muſt have ſurvived to the third century at leaſt, not only diſtinct from, but even oppoſed to, the Gael; or they would not have been mentioned ſo frequently, under their own name of Belgæ, in the Poems of Oſſian. And they accordingly appear in Mr. Macpherſon's own Temora, waging long and bloody wars with the Gael.

That the Belgæ were loſt in the Gael at all, is inferred evidently from the Iriſh, the Belgic and the Caelic Iriſh, equally calling themſelves, and being called by others, the Gael. But the inference is groſsly unjuſt. I have already ſhewn all the Belgæ of Britain to have been actually denominated Gael. And the Belgic language appears deciſively to have been the Gallic or Britiſh.

tish. This is plain from the only remains that we have of the Belgic, the names of their tribes, their towns, their woods, and their rivers, and the exact correspondency of all to the names of the British. Thus we have Isca, the name of a river among the Belgæ of Devonshire and the Britons of Wales; Alauna, for a river in Hampshire, Warwicshire, and Lancashire; and a Sturius in Kent and between Norfolk and Suffolk: the town of Camulodunum among the Belgæ of Essex and the Britons of Yorkshire; Durobrovis in Kent, and Durocobrivis in Northamptonshire; Venta in Hampshire, Norfolk, and Monmouthshire; and Vectis in Hampshire, and Vect-urion-es in Scotland: a Caledonian Wood in Kent and Sussex, in Lincolnshire and some adjoining counties, and in the Highlands of Scotland: the Damnonii of Devonshire and Valentia; the Cantæ of Caledonia, and the Cantii of Kent; and the Novantes of Middlesex and Galloway.

The whole of this passage is obviously composed, in order to give the Caledonians the honour of being the ancestors of the Irish. For this, history and reason are distorted. For this, Mr. Macpherson is at war with himself. And, for this, even Ossian is contradicted. But, even if the fact was as Mr. Macpherson states it to have been, the end and design, poor and trifling as it is, could not be answered. Even though the Belgæ had been lost in the Gael, and even though the

Gael

Gael had been Caledonians, the Caledonians could in no sense be reckoned the *sole* progenitors of the old Irish. The Irish must even then be derived from a mixt race of Britons; and the Belgæ of South-Britain must have concurred with the Gael of the North, to claim the honour of producing them. Though the Belgæ had been covered with the name of Gael, they would not less have been Belgæ, or have less contributed to produce the Irish.

P. 55—57. " When the Gael arrived first in
" Ireland they naturally gave it the name of Iar-
" in, or the western country —. From Iar-in is
" not only to be deduced the Eirin of the Irish
" themselves, but those various names by which
" the Greeks and Romans distinguished their
" island (Juverna, Ierna, Iris, Ουερνια, Hibernia).
" —Hibernia, the most common name by which
" the Romans distinguished Ireland, may appear
" to some too remote in the pronunciation and
" orthography from Iar-in, or H'Eirin [*the*
" Western Country], to be derived from either.
" This difficulty is easily removed. Julius Cæsar
" mentions, for the first time, Ireland under the
" name of Hibernia. One of two reasons in-
" duced the illustrious writer to use that appel-
" lation. He either latinized the H'Yverdhon of

" the Southern Britains, or, what is more proba-
" ble, he annexed to Ireland a name which suited
" his own ideas of its air and climate,—and—
" formed the name of Hibernia from the adjec-
" tive Hibernus."

I have cited this paffage, principally to mark the ftrange manner in which, within a few lines, the author palpably contradicts himfelf. And I have produced more than one inftance of this before.—In the beginning of the Extract, Hibernia is without hefitation pronounced to be derived from the Caledonian Iar-in. But, in the conclufion, it is declared to be derived either from the Welfh H'Yverdhon or the Latin Hibernus. Thus is Mr. Macpherfon his own greateft adverfary. And while, in the gaiety of indifcretion, he is brandifhing his fword to hew down all oppofition, he unhappily buries it in his own bofom.

The deduction of Hibernia from the Latin Hibernus is one of the meaneft and moft frivolous etymons, among the thoufands which have difgraced the fcience of etymology, that I ever remember to have feen of late. It is only fit for that infantine period of human learning and human underftanding, which originally gave it to the world, and which exhaufted all its feeble powers in the derivation of Scotland from the Greek Σκοῖος, and of Albion and Hibernia from the Latin Hibernus and Albus. And I am aftonifhed that

that a gentleman, of Mr. Macpherson's spirit and intellect, could ever stoop to raise such an etymon from its peaceful grave in the dust.

The names of Iris, Ierna, Juverna, and Hibernia are all obviously deduced from the same radical word. Iar or Eir, West, evidently forms the Ir in Iris and the Ier in Ierna. And Ier being sometimes pronounced Iver and Hiber, as Cumri and Cimmerii were changed into Cumbri and Cimbri, and as Eure, the name of a river in France and in England, was formed into Ebur in Ebur-acum and Eburo-vices; with the addition of In, an island, it plainly composes Ier-ina, Ier-na, Iver-na, and Hiber-nia.

I have here given the reader a full and compleat view of Mr. Macpherson's conjectures and arguments, concerning the first population of Ireland by the Caledonians. And the whole resolves itself into two points, That Ireland would naturally be first peopled from the Mulls of Galloway and Cantire; and, That the indigenous name of Gael for the Irish is a proof of their Caledonian descent. The former obviously

amounts

amounts only to a fair probability. And the latter has not even that merit. The argument has been repeatedly overthrown, by shewing the appellation of Gael not to have been confined to the Caledonians, but to have extended with the colonies of the Britons over all their islands. And even the probability, fair as it is, can be of no service to Mr. Macpherson, since Galloway is not within the limits of Caledonia, and since the probability is equally favourable to Galloway as to Cantire.

In the History of Manchester I have shewn from indisputable authorities, when and by whom the isle of Ireland was first inhabited. About 350 years before Christ, the Belgæ crossed the Channel into Britain, and seized the whole extended line of the southern coast from Kent into Devonshire. Numbers of the former inhabitants, that had gradually retired before the enemy, were obliged at last to take shipping upon our western coast, and passed over into the uninhabited isle of Ireland. And these were afterwards joined by another body of Britons, at the great attack upon the neighbouring states by the Belgæ under Divitiacus, who pursued the track of their brethren, and associated with them in Ireland. The first population of that fine island, therefore, was originally begun, not by the northern, but by the southern, Britons; not from the

the promontories of Caledonia, but from the shores of the Channel; in consequence of the Belgic invasion of Britain, and about the year 350 before the Christian æra. And this, the first colony that came into Ireland, was succeeded by another, which was as little deduced from the northern Britons or the hills of Caledonia, and came equally from the shores of the southern sea, in consequence of the advances of the Belgæ into the interiors of Britain, and about the year 100 before Christ[1].

I have also shewn from the same indisputable authorities, that Ireland, for two centuries and a half afterwards, was continually recruited with fresh colonies from Britain; as the populousness of this island, and the vicinity of that, invited them to settle in the one, or as the bloody and successive wars in Britain, during this period, naturally induced them to relinquish the other. The third and fourth colonies that settled in Ireland, as I have observed in the History of Manchester, were in all probability derived from Galloway and Cantire. As the Epidii and Damnii of those countries lay the nearest of any Britons to the isle of Ireland, they must therefore be supposed, after the extraordinary embarkations of their southern brethren, to have been the

[1] See History of Manchester, p. 432, 433.

first of all the Britons that planted colonies within it. And the name of Damnii, for a tribe on the opposite shores of Ireland and Britain, gives a great additional weight to the supposition. These settlements were most probably occasioned by the mere populousness of Britain, crouded as it now began to be with inhabitants, and by the mere proximity of Ireland, plain as it appeared to the eye from the shores of Cantire and Galloway. But the succeeding colonies were occasioned by the wars of the Britons among themselves, and of the Romans against them all. And I have endeavoured, and with no little success, I think, to trace back every new colony to its original district in Britain, and to refer their passage into Ireland to the very commotion that sent them thither. The island appears to have been planted with colonies from the whole range of our western coast. The Belgæ of Dorsetshire and Cornwall at one end, the Britons of Caledonia at the other, and almost every nation betwixt them, all contributed to the population of Ireland. And the whole circuit of the country was compleatly peopled about 150 years after Christ. Some historical notices, that have never been made use of before, have lent the general light that has directed me in this discovery. The occurrence of the same names of tribes and of towns, in both islands, has led me on. One or two

two intimations and some historical facts, in the Poems of Ossian, have furnished additional evidence. And from the whole I have been enabled to draw up the first authentic history of Ireland, as to the primary population of the isle, and the original transactions of the colonists, that has hitherto made its appearance in any language¹.

---

¹ See History of Manchester, p. 434—438.

CHAP.

CHAP. III.

WE are now come to that important period of Mr. Macpherson's Introduction, for which all the rest was evidently written, for which we have seen all the annals of the island and the continent distorted from their true line, antient History garbled and contradicted, and Mr. Macpherson's own assertions mangled and opposed. We are now come to the Origin of the Scots.

I.

FROM p. 58 to 78 Mr. Macpherson is engaged in a formal attack upon the pretenfions of the Irifh, to an original very different from the other inhabitants of the Britifh ifles, in order to prove them and the Scots the defcendants of the Caledonians. The attack indeed is very eafy. Thofe fabricks of fiction, which the Irifh credulity and patriotifm have been rearing for ages, all melt away before the ftrong beams of Hiftory and Criticifm. But the romances are replete with fuch prodigies of fiction and folly, and are fo univerfally defpifed by the judicious and the thinking both on the continent and in our own ifland, that they were not worthy of a ferious refutation. And fuch a writer as Mr. Macpherfon, engaged in fuch a conteft, feems to me like the redoubtable Sir John in Shakefpear, attacking a dead man fword in hand, and with one wound more in his thigh carrying him away in triumph[1].

[1] But it is proper to obferve, that almoft every argument in this difquifition is borrowed, fometimes literally, and generally without acknowledgement, from Innes's Critical Eflay. The reference to Strabo in p. 60 and 61 of Mr. Macpherfon; to Mela, Tacitus, and Solinus, in p. 62; the anfwers to objec-

Mr. Macpherson in p. 78—91 applies himself to the harder task of refuting the arguments of Father Innes, concerning the Spanish or the Scandinavian extraction of the Scots of Ireland. But these, and all the other conclusions of our Historians and Antiquarians, may be answered without any great difficulty. Fluttering for want of information concerning the real descent of the Scots, the historical mind has wandered over the continent in search of their original home, has eagerly caught at the most trifling appearances of argument, has readily embraced the wildest suggestions of Tradition, and has molded both into a system, which is more specious and solid than the fictions of the Irish, but which easily yields to the pressure of a well-directed blow. So far therefore as Mr. Macpherson's arguments relate only to the Spanish or Scandinavian origin of the Scots, I shall not attend to them. Mr. Macpherson may demolish those Gothick Structures at his will. His efforts are spirited, and his labours decisive. But when he endeavours, as he does

tions in p. 63; the appeal to Camden, Ware, and Usher, in p. 64, 65; what is said of Ware and the Psalter-Cashel in p. 67, and of the form of the Irish Alphabet in p. 67, 68; are all taken from Innes p. 428, 429, 431, and 432, 430, 433—434, 435—437, 434—435, 439, and 448—449, without one acknowledgement of the real Owner, and more than once with the adoption of his own words.—And Dr. Macpherson had borrowed some of the arguments before from Innes. See p. 88—90.—Compare also p. 70, 71 of Mr. Macpherson with p. 90 of Dr. Macpherson.

twice,

twice, to derive any advantage from his conquests in favour of a Caledonian origin, I muft then beg leave to interpofe, and fhew his pretenfions to be as falfe as the Irifh, and his arguments as vifionary as Innes's.

P. 78, 79. At entering on his refutation, Mr. Macpherfon fpeaks thus.—" They [the " Scots] came, fays the ingenious Father [Innes], " either from Scandia or Cantabria [into Ire- " land], about the time of the Incarnation, or " rather a little time after it.—Innes is the only " writer who has reduced the origin of the Scots " into a regular fyftem; and he endeavours to " defend it. Should the ingenious Father's " fcheme be deftroyed, the Caledonian extraction " of the Irifh muft of courfe rife upon its ruins."

This is furely a very extraordinary argument. Though the Irifh be proved not to have been derived from Scandinavia or Cantabria, we are not one ftep nearer to their derivation from Caledonia. They may have come with equal probability from the whole extended fhore of Britain, that reaches from Caledonia to the Channel. And I have already fhewn that they actually did.

P. 90,

P. 90, 91. At the conclusion of his refutation, Mr. Macpherson speaks thus.—" We must " have recourse, in the last resort, to the Cale- " donian Britons for the genuine origin of the " Irish. Their name of Gael, their language, " the conformity of their manners and customs " with those of the Old Britons, all concur in " proving, beyond any possibility of reply, that " the Irish are the posterity of the Gauls or " Gael, who, after having traversed the island " of Great Britain, passed over, in a very early " period, into Ireland from the promontories of " Galloway and Cantire."

All the arguments here hinted at have been urged before. And I shall not re-answer them here.—I have frequently remarked before Mr. Macpherson's repeated inconsistency, in sometimes extending his Caledonia on the south to the Wall of Severus, and in sometimes reducing it to the Friths of Forth and Clyde. And I have also observed, that, as the real Caledonia never included Galloway, no argument, for the passage of the first colonists into Ireland from Galloway, will evince the Caledonian descent of the Irish.— I have repeatedly shewn above, that the name of Gael cannot assist in proving the Irish to be the posterity of the Caledonians. It will equally prove them to have been the posterity of the Gallowese, the Welsh, and the Cornish, and of any tribe in any part of this island.—The correspondency

respondency of language, manners, and customs, betwixt the Irish and Caledonians, is just as good an argument as the community of names before. The language, manners, and customs, of almost all the interior Islanders, have been shewn to be exactly the same.—But the author's management of his argument, with regard to the correspondency of manners and customs, is a little observable. " We must have recourse," says He, " to the *Caledonian Britons* for the genuine " origin of the Irish." And one argument is, " the conformity of their [the Irish] manners " and customs with those"—,not of the Caledonian Britons, as it should obviously have been, in contradistinction to all the others, but of " the Old Britons" in general. To prove the *Caledonian* descent of the Irish, Mr. Macpherson alledges the sameness of manners in the Irish and the Old Britons.—These arguments therefore, which " all concur in proving beyond any pos- " sibility of reply," that the Irish are the posterity of the Caledonians, are all really beside the mark, and prove something very different from the point intended.

So far I have considered this passage, as it contains a repetition of former arguments. I will now consider it, as an inference from the reply to Father Innes. And, as such, it is in the same strain precisely with the quotation before. Like that, it forgets an intermediate link in the chain

chain of reasoning. What Mr. Macpherson has said, disproves the Spanish and Scandinavian descent of the Irish. And so far it is useful. But it then contends for another, which is just as imaginary as the system of the Fileas or the Hypothesis of the Jesuit. And, in the love of innovation and the prevalence of prejudice, Mr. Macpherson has over-looked the obvious tendency of his own arguments, and substituted Caledonia for Britain.

P. 92. Mr. Macpherson now proceeds regularly to overthrow the Irish descent of the Scots, and to establish the Caledonian. And I shall attend him regularly in his progress.

P. 92. "The credit of the Milesian tale is
" already destroyed, and it is perhaps super-
" fluous to refute the pretended Hibernian ex-
" traction of the Scots. Both stories depend
" upon the same authority, and they must both
" fall by the same argument."

This is certainly not true. The Milesian story concerning the first population of Ireland, and the account of the migration of the Scots from Ireland into Britain, are two incidents that are
founded

founded upon very different authorities. The former rests solely upon the credit of writers that never existed, and upon the authority of records that were written some ages before the use of Letters was known in the island. The latter is grounded upon the authority of writers actually or nearly cotemporary with the facts, upon histories of the best credit, and upon records of the greatest authenticity, Bede, Orosius, and others. And this our author sufficiently acknowledges hereafter. In p. 110 he says, that " the abet-" tors of the Hibernian Antiquities, finding that " the credit of the domestic annals of Ireland " could never establish this fact, had recourse " to some passages of foreign writers." The Hibernian extraction of the Scots therefore, according to Mr. Macpherson himself, does not " depend upon the same authority" with the Milesian tale, and must not " fall by the same " argument." It is fixed, according to Mr. Macpherson himself, upon the additional testimonies " of foreign writers;" and it must be overthrown by a reply to those testimonies. And Mr. Macpherson accordingly cites the authority of Claudian, Orosius, Isidore, and Bede for it, in p. 105, 111, 116, &c., and spends various pages in replying to them. So little does the author seem to have had a full view of his plan, as he proceeded in the work. And so little does he seem to have looked back upon the parts, when he had compleated the whole.

P. 93. "It has already appeared that nothing certain is known concerning the affairs of Ireland, prior to the miſſion of St. Patrick."

This is a reference to the preceding parts of the work. And, what is very extraordinary, it is directly contradictory to them.—We are here told, that nothing certain is known concerning the affairs of Ireland before the days of St. Patrick. And yet in p. 80 Mr. Macpherſon himſelf argues from Diodorus, that the Iriſh were Britons; in p. 81 (and again in p. 95) from Tacitus, that in the days of Agricola the Iriſh were ſo weak, as to be deemed a ready conqueſt to a Legion and a competent number of Auxiliaries; in p. 82 from Ptolemy, that the Velaborii, Brigantes, Caucii, and Menapii were ſome of the tribes of Ireland; in p. 60, 61, 62, and 63, from Strabo, Diodorus, Mela, and Solinus, that the Iriſh were then rude and uncivilized; and in p. 63 (and again in p. 95) from Tacitus, that in his time the Iriſh ports were even more frequented by the merchants, and were therefore better known to the world, than the Britiſh.

It

It gives me pain to remark the grofs and repeated contradictions in fo ingenious a writer. I ftrain, I exaggerate, nothing. I only collate parts with parts. And the inconfiftency, that appears upon the face of thefe collations, muft be attributed, fometimes to Mr. Macpherfon's fervility to the interefts of an Hypothefis, and fometimes to the haftinefs and inattention with which Mr. Macpherfon appears to have written his work.

II.

THE author, now fetting himfelf to prove, that no Irifh colony tranfmigrated into Britain in or after the reign of Domitian, takes a review of what the Romans have communicated to us concerning the ftate of Caledonia, from that period to the appearance of the Scots on the frontiers of the province. With this review I am but partially concerned: Till it defcends to the 4th century, it has no relation to that migration of the Scots into Ireland, which alone is afserted in the History of Manchester and I wish to defend. And I shall therefore, in pursuing Mr. Macpherson's steps here, only mark occasionally some of the more important mistakes, till he has deduced the history to the proper period.

P. 99. " The incursions of the Caledonians " rendered it necessary for that Emperor [Adrian] to come in person into Britain; but that " the Barbarians suffered very little loss by his " arms we may naturally infer, from his relinquishing to them all that tract of country which " extends from the Tine and Solway to the " Scottish Friths."

That the incursions of the Caledonians rendered it necessary for Adrian to come into Britain, is not true. And that he relinquished all the country from the Tine and the Solway to the Friths, is a mistake.—Adrian went into all the provinces of the Empire. Romanum orbem circuivit, says Florus with an expressive elegance. Was this occasioned by the Caledonian incursions? He only visited Britain, as he visited Gaul and the other dominions of the Romans.— Nor did he relinquish Valentia to the Caledonians, by building a Wall from Solway to the Tine. This I have fully shewn in the History of Manchester. And all the region of Valentia remained in the poffeffion of the Romans, to the period of their departure from Britain [1].

P. 100. " Lollius Urbicus, in the reign of
" Antoninus Pius, defeated the Caledonians; and,
" driving them beyond the Forth and Clyde,
" excluded them by an earthen Wall from the
" Roman Britain. Though repelled by Urbi-
" cus,—they were far from being reduced fo low
" as to yield a part of their territories to the Ro-
" mans."

This is a great miftake. The Brigantes, or Caledonians, are exprefsly faid by Paufanias to have loft a confiderable tract of country, $\tau\eta\nu$ $\pi o\lambda\lambda\eta\nu$, to the Romans at this period. And I have fully fhewn in the Hiftory of Manchefter, that this confifted of half the region of Caledonia [2].

P. 101, 102. " Severus — marched north-
" ward, with a fixed refolution to exterminate the
" whole nation of the Caledonians. But—he
" was at laft reduced to the old and inglorious
" expedient of building a Wall to exclude from

[1] Hiftory of Manchefter, p. 453—458.
[2] P. 454—461, and 418, 419.

" the Province thofe Barbarians whom he could
" neither extirpate or fubdue. (Ες φιλιαν επαγηλ-
" θεν, ες ομολογιαν τας Βρετ]ανας επι τω χωρας αχ
" ολιγης εχςηναι, αναγκασας ελθειν. Dion. Caff.
" lib. 76)."

This is in general a very unfair reprefentation of the principles and fuccefs of Severus's expedition. And it will eafily appear, even from Mr. Macpherfon himfelf, to be unfair.—It is here exprefsly declared, that Severus could not fubdue any of the Caledonians. And it is here plainly implied, that he relinquifhed to them all the country to the North of his Wall. " He " was—reduced to the *old* and *inglorious* expe-" dient of building a Wall to exclude from *the* " *Province* thofe Barbarians whom he could nei-" ther extirpate or *fubdue*." But Severus actually fubdued all the tribes of the Mæatæ, and pretty certainly recovered all the conquefts of Lollius'. And the very quotation, which Mr. Macpherfon adduces in proof of his own pofition, exprefsly declares the contrary. The quotation fays pofitively, that Severus forced the Caledonians to refign up no fmall portion of their country to him, χωρας αχ ολιγης εχςηναι. And this concurs with many inftances before to fhew us, how little dependence we can have upon Mr. Macpherfon's authorities, even when

' See Hiftory of Manchefter, p. 419.

he recites them fairly at the foot of the page, and when he has no ſtrong bias to miſlead his hand as he copies.—Nor did Severus relinquiſh Valentia to the Caledonians. When he was advancing with a reſolution to reduce all Caledonia, or when he was juſt returning from the actual reduction of half the country, he could not poſſibly have been either compelled or invited to reſign up Valentia to the enemy. And Valentia remained one of the 5 Provinces of Roman Britain, to the final period of the Roman dominion in the iſland [1].—Nor was the reſolution to exterminate the Caledonians taken up by Severus, before he made his expedition into their country. It was taken up afterwards, when the ſubjected tribes of Caledonia had thrown off their obedience, and were inſtantly joined by the reſt of the Caledonians. Severus's reſentment kindled at the news. He ordered the army immediately, and in the depth of winter, to march to the North under the command of Caracalla, to relieve the garriſons in the ſtations [2], which muſt have been cloſely beſieged, and to ſpread an univerſal carnage through the country. And Mr. Macpherſon has attributed a deſign to the firſt expedition, which was only an order for the ſecond [3].

[1] Hiſtory of Mancheſter, p. 454. [2] Dio, p. 1287, τα φρυρια. [3] Hiſtory of Mancheſter, p. 419, 420.

P. 94—104. In these pages is contained the first great argument, " to prove that no Irish " colony tranfmigrated into Britain in or after " the reign of Domitian" (p. 94). And in p. " 103, 104. we are told thus.—" In the long " period which intervened between the acceffion of " the fons of Severus to the Imperial dignity, and " the middle of the 4th age,—the frequent contefts " for the purple,—the public diftractions which " arofe naturally from thefe difputes, the growing " imbecillity of the Empire, and the invafions of " the Barbarians of the northern Europe, di- " verted the attention of the Romans from Ca- " ledonia. In a period fo long, and of fuch " tranquillity, the inhabitants of North Britain, " inftead of declining, muft have greatly multi- " plied their numbers. In the tenth Conſulſhip " of Conftantius, the fon of Conftantine, we " meet with the Scots, a formidable Nation in " Britain. Ammianus Marcellinus, who found " them firſt in the ifland, does not furnifh one ob- " fcure hint that they derived their blood from a " foreign country."

This long argument is intended to prove two points; That, in all this period of time, from the reign of Domitian to the middle of the fourth age, the Caledonians were never reduced fo

much

much, as to have any part of their country rent from them by a colony from Ireland; and, That, when the Scots are firſt mentioned as in the iſland by Marcellinus, he does not hint that they derived their deſcent from a foreign country. This is the full ſum and ſubſtance of the argument. And it is evidently unſatisfactory. To prove that no colony *tranſmigrated* from Ireland into Britain, he endeavours to ſhew, that no Iriſh colony *ſettled* in Britain by *violence*. To *prove* that the Scots did not come into Britain from Ireland, he ſhews that the hiſtorian, who firſt mentions them in Britain, does not ſay that they came from Ireland. The former is a mere fallacy, the ſubſtitution of one term for another. And the latter is merely a negative argument, ſtrangely adduced in ſupport of a poſitive aſſertion.

To this clear and ſhort refutation of Mr. Macpherſon's great argument, it is proper to add one obſervation concerning the alledged ſilence of Marcellinus. He who firſt found the Scots in this iſland, it is ſaid, " does not furniſh one ob-
" ſcure hint that they derived their blood from
" a foreign country." But Mr. Macpherſon is not aware, that the part of Marcellinus's hiſtory, which firſt noticed the Scots as in Britain, has been long loſt to the world. The appearance of the Scots " in the tenth conſulſhip of Conſtan-
" tius," is not the firſt that they made in the
                                                                Hiſtory

History of Marcellinus. They made one twenty years before it, and in that portion of the history which has been unhappily destroyed. Consulatu — Constantii decies, terque Juliani, in Britanniis cum *Scotorum* Pictorumque, gentium ferarum, excursus, ruptâ quiete *condictâ,* loca limitibus vicina vastarent, et implicaret formido Provincias *præteritarum cladium* congerie *fessas;* hiemem agens apud Parisios, Cæsar — verebatur *ire subsidio transmarinis,* ut *retulimus ante fecisse Constantem* [1]. Here we are informed, that the Scots and Picts had recently ravaged the country before 360, that Constans had passed over to repel them, and that Marcellinus had given an account of both these incidents. And Marcellinus appears to have taken occasion from that incursion into the province, to have expatiated in a long and laboured description of the country that was then invaded, and to have given a particular account of the Scots and Picts that invaded it. Quoniam, says he himself, cùm Constantis Principis acta componerem, motus adolescentis & senescentis oceani, situmque Britanniæ, pro captu virium explanavi, ad ea quæ digesta sunt semel, revolvi superfluum duxi — : illud tamen sufficiet dici, quod eo tempore Picti—itidemque Attacotti —, et Scotti, per diversa vagantes multa populabantur [2]. And therefore for

[1] L. xx. c. 1. [2] L. xxvii. c. 8.

Mr. Macpherson to affirm, that Marcellinus, who first found the Scots in Britain, furnishes not one obscure hint of their derivation from a foreign country; is to mistake the time when Marcellinus first finds them in the island, is to assert what is certainly not true, and is to adduce an argument in favour of the Caledonian extraction of the Scots, which is equally frivolous in its nature and false in its attestation.

III.

PAG. 105. "Bede is the first writer who
"positively affirms that the Scots of Britain
"derived their origin from those of Ireland.
"Whether they originally obtained from the
"Picts the principality of — Argyle by force or
"treaty, was a point which all his historical and
"traditional knowledge did not enable the vene-
"rable Anglo-Saxon to determine. The inca-
"pacity of Bede, who lived so near the pre-
"tended

"tended tranfmigration of the Irifh, to folve this
"difficulty, is a kind of demonftration that the
"whole ftory is a fiction, impofed upon that cre-
"dulous, though pious writer."

This is furely fuch an argument as was never produced before againft a refpectable hiftorian. And it would furely be of no avail at all, even againft the moft irrefpectable that ever difgraced the file of hiftorical writers.—Bede's unacquaintednefs with the reafons and principles of a great tranfaction, can never annihilate his credit with regard to the fact itfelf. Such a great national tranfaction, as the firft fettlement of a body of Irifh Scots on the coaft of Caledonia, is an incident equally notorious and remarkable, that is not only obvious to all that are within the fphere of obfervation, but calls and compels the attention of all the nations immediately about. The reafon of the fact, however, lies much deeper, and is generally known only to the more informed and more inquifitive part of the obfervers. The one therefore is naturally recorded by many writers. But the other is given only by fuch, as look beyond the furface of the incident, and fearch for the fprings that operated to produce it. And even hiflorians that are cotemporary with a fact, and that even endeavour to affign the reafon and principle of it, are frequently unable, for want of proper information, to afcertain the true one; and different writers

attribute

attribute the same incident to different causes. From some of the many, Bede and Richard transcribed the account which they have given us; and the latter, as I have already shewn in the History of Manchester, happily met with the year of the deed precisely ascertained[1]. But neither of them found any historian, that had investigated the actuating motive and principle of it. That is left to the conjectural criticisms of later writers. And in the History of Manchester I have guessed at a motive, which has several coincidences of reason and history in its favour, and is therefore in all probability the true and genuine principle[2].

P. 105, 106. " If the Picts were so feeble that
" a band of Irish adventurers could tear from
" them one third of their dominions, how came
" they so frequently to provoke the Roman legions,
" and harass the provincials from the
" time of Chlorus to the total dereliction of Britain
" by Honorius? To invade the territories
" of a warlike and disciplined people when they
" suffered a great part of their own to be wrested
" from them by a despicable enemy, is a folly

[1] P. 446.   [2] P. 447.

"too abfurd to gain any credit. But perhaps the Picts gave the diftrict of Argyle to their allies of Ireland, in confideration of fervices againft the Romans. Thefe fervices were extremely unneceffary; for the Romans, till provoked by incurfions, were very inoffenfive towards the Barbarians beyond the walls. Nations, in fhort, have been known to receive foreigners into the bofom of their country to repel invafions, but it is ridiculous to think that any people would have recourfe to fo dangerous an expedient for the pleafure of haraffing neighbours who did not in any degree offend them."

The former was Mr. Macpherfon's firft argument againft Bede. This is his fecond. And it is calculated to prove, that the Scots could not have fettled in Caledonia, either by force or by treaty. But, fuppofing every part of the argument to be juft, the whole is of no moment at all againft a fact, that is pofitively afferted by a credible authority. Such an argument would not deftroy the flighteft incident of the flighteft hiftory that ever was written. Though the Scots could not fettle by force, as indeed I think that Mr. Macpherfon's reafoning feems ftrongly to evince, they might fettle by treaty, for any reafon that is affigned by Mr. Macpherfon. The fervices of the Scots againft the Romans might be unneceffary: and yet the Caledonians might allow

allow them a portion of land in their country. To invite the Irish into the island, merely to attack the inoffensive Romans, might be folly in the Caledonians; and yet they might do it. Mr. Macpherson forgets, that he is arguing, not against the assigned reasons of a fact, but against the existence of the fact itself. Against the former his arguments would carry weight. But they carry none at all against the latter. There are also other modes of settling peaceably in a country, than what is here mentioned. And in the History of Manchester I have suggested one very different from this, and in all probability the true one [1].

P. 106, 107.—It is difficult for the unpre-
" judiced part of mankind to believe, that a
" colony, sufficient to occupy the western high-
" lands and isles, could have wafted themselves,
" their wives, and children, at once, from Ireland
" into the northern Britain, in Curraghs or
" miserable skiffs, whose hulls of wicker were
" wrapped up in a cow's hide. In these wretch-
" ed vessels, it is true, an irregular communi-
" cation was kept up between both the islands;
" but the navigation was dangerous, and per-

[1] P. 447.

" formed

"formed only in the fairest days of summer,
"(Mare quod Britanniam et Hiberniam inter-
"luit, undosum et inquietum, toto in anno non
"nisi æstivis pauculis diebus est navigabile: navi-
"gant autem vimineis alveis quos circumdant
"ambitione tergorum bubulinorum. Solin. xxxv.).
"The fertility of the soil of Iar-ghael [Argyle]
"could never be an inducement to an Irish
"migration into that division of Caledonia. If
"poverty, or their being overstocked with num-
"bers, compelled the inhabitants of the pre-
"tended Dalrietta, or the Route in the county of
"Antrim, to go in quest of foreign settlements,
"they ought in common prudence to have tried
"their fortune in the southern division of their
"own country, and not in the sterile mountains of
"the western Caledonia [1]."

In making these Extracts, I am obliged to tran-
scribe Mr. Macpherson line by line, in order to
give each argument its full play, and to act ho-
nourably with him and the reader. And each
argument, like this, is a mere Sorites, an accumulation of little reasons, that, inconsiderable in
themselves, may appear important in their
union. But, in order to answer the whole, I must
reduce it into its constituent parts, examine each

---

[1] So Sir G. Mackenzie, p. 375 and 405, vol. i. asserts the Irish sea to have been generally not navigable in curraghs, and also quotes Solinus for it.

separately,

separately, and then see the joint result of all.

The import of the first position is, that no colony of Irish could have migrated into Caledonia, because their vessels were so slight and the navigation so dangerous. This is directly pointed against the assertion of Bede. And, could the position be proved, the assertion must be given up.—But, in order to prove it, Mr. Macpherson has introduced a foreign circumstance into the fact. And he argues, that no colony of Irish, *sufficient to occupy the western Highlands and isles*, could have come over *at once*. Bede does not assert, that the colony was sufficient to occupy the western Highlands and isles, whether by *occupying* Mr. Macpherson means a forcible reduction or a compleat inhabitation of them. And Mr. Macpherson is therefore arguing, not against Bede, but against some writer in nubibus. Bede says thus. Procedente — tempore Britannia, post Britones et Pictos, tertiam Scottorum nationem in Pictorum parte recepit; qui, duce Reudâ de Hiberniâ progressi, vel amicitiâ vel ferro sibimet inter eos *sedes quas hactenus habent vindicarunt* —. Est autem sinus maris permaximus, qui antiquitus gentem Britonum a Pictis secernebat, qui ab occidente in terras longo spatio erumpit, ubi est civitas Britonum munitissima usque hodie, quæ vocatur Alcluith ; *ad cujus* videlicet *sinûs partem septen-*

septentrionalem Scotti, quos diximus, advenientes, sibi locum patriæ fecerunt [1]. Bede, we see, fixes not the Scots along the western Highlands and isles, but merely upon the northern bank of the Clyde. And Mr. Macpherson, involuntarily indeed, has disguised the assertion of Bede in order to overthrow it, and has loaded it with an extraordinary circumstance to make it appear extravagant.—Nor is the declaration, concerning the nature of the vessels and the navigation, less strained or less unjust. Mr. Macpherson has misrepresented the curraghs, describing one of them as contained within the compass of a single hide. But his quotation from Solinus says no such thing: Vimineis alveis quos circumdant ambitione tergorum bubulinorum. Each boat was actually lined with several hides. Carinæ primùm ac statumina, says Cæsar, ex levi materiâ fiebant: reliquum corpus navium, viminibus contextum, coriis integebatur [2]. And for Mr. Macpherson to affirm, that the British curraghs were not sufficient to transport over a body of men from Ireland, is at once to oppose himself, to deny half the facts in his own Ossian, and to contradict the express declarations of history. In p. 225 Mr. Macpherson assures us, that " the size of those " vessels must have been greater than is generally

[1] L. i. c. 1.   [2] P. 240.

" supposed,

"suppofed, for the Saxon auxiliaries of Vorti-
"gern tranfported themfelves in three of them
"from Germany to Britain." And, in the preceding parts of the work, we have feen Mr.
Macpherfon fuppofing colonies to have paffed
over from Gaul into Britain, and from Caledonia
into Ireland. -Indeed the whole of the author's
hiftorical fyftem, before, is founded upon the
fuppofition. And thofe colonies muft certainly
have paffed over in curraghs, as thefe were the
only veffels of the Britons¹. The Irifh of the
fourth century could not poffibly be more uncivilized, more unexperienced in the arts of
navigation, than their anceftors many ages before; efpecially as their ports, according to Mr.
Macpherfon himfelf in p. 95, were fo particularly frequented by the merchants, even in the
firft century. And if the great colonies of Mr.
Macpherfon's Gael, his Cimbri, and his Belgæ,
colonies fufficient to occupy all Caledonia, all
Maxima and Britannia Secunda, and all Britannia Prima and Flavia, if thefe could migrate in
curraghs into Britain, and if thefe could migrate
afterwards into Ireland in fufficient numbers to
occupy the whole compafs of the ifland; the
Irifh could certainly remigrate in them as well to
the coaft of Caledonia, and even in numbers
fufficient to occupy the weftern Highlands and

¹ Cæfar, p. 240, and Pliny, l. iv. c. 16.

isles. In Mr. Macpherson's own Ossian also, as I have already observed in the History of Manchester [1], we see little armies continually transported in these vessels from Caledonia to Ireland, and from Ireland to Caledonia. And as the first colonists of Britain must necessarily have wafted over the intermediate channels in curraghs, so in Gildas we see the Picts and Scots of the fifth century hastily crossing the Friths of Forth and Clyde in their curraghs [2]; we find the Britons of the first expressly declared by Lucan, to have navigated the seas about them in their curraghs [3]; succours were sent in curraghs from South-Britain into Gaul, in the days of Caesar [4]; and a great army was transported in curraghs, even by Caesar himself, across the very rapid current of the Sicoris in Spain [5]. These facts equally demonstrate, against Mr. Macpherson, the sufficiency of the British curraghs for the embarkation of

[1] P. 381.

[2] Hist. c. xv. Emergunt certatim de Curicis, qnibus sunt trans Tithicam vallem vecti.

[3] Sic Venetus stagnante Pado, fusoque Britannus Oceano. And Pliny says thus in l. iv. c. 16. Timæus historicus a Britannia introrsus sex dierum navigatione abesse dicit insulam Mictim —, ad eam Britannos vitilibus navigiis corio circumfutis navigare.

[4] Cæsar, p. 73, Omnibus fere Gallicis bellis, hostibus nostris inde subministrata auxilia intelligebat.

[5] Milites his navibus flumen transportat, Cæsar, p. 240.

armies,

armies, and evince, against Solinus, the general navigableness of the Irish channel by them. If these sea-boats could live in the channel between Gaul and Britain, they could equally live in the sea betwixt Britain and Ireland. If these curraghs could cross the British Channel laden with troops, they could equally in the same circumstances cross the Irish. If, thus laden, they were able to stem the heady current of a narrow river, swelled with all the melting snows of the mountains¹; they must have been equally able to stem the current of St. George's channel. And we accordingly see them in Ossian, as I have observed before, perpetually passing from Ireland to Caledonia and from Caledonia to Ireland².

Thus is one great part of this argument answered. And this, indeed, is by much the strongest. The other is, That no colony of Irish could have been induced to settle in Argyle, because of its natural barrenness. But this sort

---

¹ Cæsar, p. 237.

² In Ossian, vol. ii. p. 212 Mr. Macpherson himself observes thus: "One thing is certain, that the Caledonians *often* made their way through the dangerous and tempestuous seas of Scandinavia, which is more, perhaps, than the more polished nations, subsisting in those times, dared to venture." And Mr. Macpherson makes the Caledonians the ancestors of the Irish.

of problematical arguments may be propagated ad infinitum, and equally on either side of an historical question. And they are of no consequence at all, either way, as to the fact. The Scots may have passed over into the western Caledonia, though the fertility of the country could be no inducement. The Irish of Dalrieta may have settled in Argyle, though the south of Ireland was more attracting. And History expressly assures us that they did.

P. 107. "The Irish must have been wonder-"fully improved in military knowledge from the "days of Agricola, if it was more difficult [for "the Irish of Dalrieta] in the fourth century to "extort part of their dominions from them, than "from the Caledonians, who had better oppor-"tunities to be enured to arms."

This argument is directed only against the supposition, of the Scots settling by force in Caledonia. But that is too improbable in itself, to be supposed by any who are conversant with the histories of Caledonia and Ireland. And it stands directly refuted by the well-known concurrence of the Caledonians and the Irish settlers, in incursions into the Roman Province, within a few years only after the settlement. The great point

at

at which Mr. Macpherson should direct his arguments is, That the Irish could not have fixed themselves in Argyle by the consent of the Caledonians. And for this purpose he should specify all the various modes of settling amicably in a country, and shew the impossibility, or at least the high improbability, of each of these with respect to the Caledonians and the Irish.

P. 107, 108. " Should it be supposed that a
" band of adventurers were expelled from Ulster
" by the pressure of the Southern Irish, it is
" difficult to account how the Picts of Britain
" should receive the fugitives. Either generosity
" or selfishness would have prompted them — to
" assist the exiles in recovering their territories,
" and, by that means, to endeavour to conquer a
" part of a fine country for themselves. But the
" Picts were, it seems, strangers to the most com-
" mon maxims of policy; for, according to the
" system under consideration, they must have
" been of all nations the most tame, prodigal, and
" imprudent."

This is exactly in the same tenour and spirit, as one or two arguments before. The Caledonians might be of all nations the most tame, prodigal, and imprudent, if the fact was true: and yet the fact, if properly authenticated, would stand unimpeached.

P. 108, 109. "The Saxon auxiliaries of
" Vortigern were not so modest as the Irish Scots;
" or else the Picts were a people of much less
" spirit than the southern Britons. When the
" Saxons raised their demands to an unreasonable
" height, the Britons disputed with them every
" inch of ground —. Had the Hibernian merce-
" naries encroached upon the Picts, as the Sax-
" ons did on the Britons, we might naturally
" suppose that the latter [the Picts], instead of
" carrying war and desolation into a foreign
" country, in conjunction with the Scots, would
" have found employment for their arms at
" home. The unanimity in expedition which
" subsisted for ages between the Caledonian
" nations, is proof sufficient that they derived
" their origin from one and the same source."

This is the sixth argument against Bede's assertion, of a settlement of Scots upon the western
shore of Caledonia. But it is obviously pointed
only against a settlement by violence. It is therefore of no moment against the peaceable and
amicable establishment of the Scots in Caledonia.

But

But there are some particulars mentioned in the course of the argument, which it may be proper to notice.—The author alledges the joint expeditions of the Caledonian Scots and the native Caledonians into the Roman province, as a proof that the former did not settle in the country by violence. And yet, when he draws his conclusion, he infers, not that the Scots settled amicably in Caledonia, but that the Scots and Caledonians were "of one and the same source."— He concludes them both to have been "of one "and the same source," because they associated in incursions into the Province. I have urged the argument before, in proof of the Scots settling themselves in Caledonia with the consent of the natives. And this is all that it proves. Two nations of a different source, being fixed in the same country, might naturally unite in expeditions against a common enemy.—And, what is still more remarkable, Mr. Macpherson, in the former parts of his work, has strenuously endeavoured to derive the Irish from the Caledonians; and the Scots must therefore, according to Mr. Macpherson's own system, be "of one and the "same source" with the Caledonians, even if they came over from Ireland. So little does one great part of Mr. Macpherson's system unite with another. And so little do the conclusion and the premises agree together.

THESE

THESE are the arguments, by which the authority of Bede, concerning the primary derivation of the Scots into Britain, is fuppofed to be overthrown. And each of them, it is obvious, is without the fmalleft force. The reafons urged againft an eftablifhment by violence, are convincing in themfelves, but carry no conclufivenefs in them with regard to the main point. And the reafons advanced againft an eftablifhment by confent, are all vague and frivolous. There are various kinds of amicable fettlements; and the author fhould have endeavoured to fet them all afide. But he has mentioned only one or two. And he has particularly omitted that which I have mentioned in the Hiftory of Manchefter, and which was in all probability the very kind of amicable eftablifhment, that took place upon the prefent occafion [*].

---

[*] Hiftory of Manchefter, p. 447.

IV.

IV.

HAVING now advanced his six arguments against Bede, Mr. Macpherson proceeds to overthrow the cited authorities of foreign writers. And Claudian comes first.

P. 111, 112. " That poet, in his panegyric on
" Theodosius, has the following lines,

" Quid rigor æternus cœli; quid sidera prosunt,
" Ignotumque Fretum? Maduerunt Saxone fuso
" Orcades: incaluit Pictorum sanguine Thule:
" Scottorum cumulos flevit glacialis Ierne.

" But we may venture to affirm, that there is
" nothing in this passage conclusive in favour of
" the old Milesian tale [the extraction of the Scots
" from Ireland].— It is idle — to search for fact
" in the hyperboles of poetry; Marcellinus,
" though particularly fond of Theodosius, has
" not recorded these prodigies of valour: even
" Latinus Pacatius, though a Panegyrist, says no
" more, than that the Scot was driven back to
" his

" his native fens (redactum in paludes fuas Scot-
" tum. Latin. Pacat. in Panegyr. Theod.), and
" the Saxon deftroyed in conflicts by fea. — If
" the Hibernians were of Caledonian extract; if,
" from the ancient ties of confanguinity, a friend-
" ly intercourfe was maintained between the Irish
" and the inhabitants of Albany; a perfon of a
" lefs warm imagination than Claudian might
" fuppofe that the former fincerely lamented the
" misfortunes of their mother nation."

In this argument againft the cuftomary and obvious application of the paffage in Claudian, is one thing intimated and another afferted. It is afferted, that the account in Claudian is not confirmed by any other writer, and muft therefore be confidered as the exaggeration of poetry. And it is intimated, that if Ireland was peopled from Caledonia, and if the Irish kept up a friendly intercourfe with the Caledonians, Ierne might with propriety be faid to lament the carnage of the Scots, though thefe Scots were not derived from Ireland, and though they were native Caledonians.

The affertion is not true. Latinus Pacatus, even as quoted and interpreted by Mr. Macpherfon, clearly gives us the fubftance of what Claudian has more fully opened. Latinus deftroys the Saxons " in conflicts by fea:" Claudian fixes the conflicts at the Orkney iflands;

Quid

Quid rigor æternus cœli, quid fidera profunt,
Ignotumque fretum? Maduerunt Saxone fufo
Orcades.

Latinus has omitted the Picts, who were undoubtedly and confeffedly concerned: Claudian more accurately has noticed them. Latinus drives back the Scots to their native bogs, redactum in paludes fuas; an expreffion, not fuited at all to the mountains of Argyle, but highly characteriftic of the plains of Ireland: and Claudian mentions the Scots as the fons of Ireland, and makes a great carnage of them. And where, efpecially with regard to the laft and main point, is the difference betwixt the poetical and profaical hiftorian? And where is the Hyperbole and the warm imagination of Claudian? His colouring is ftronger: but his texture is the fame as Latinus's. And it appears from both, that the Irifh at this period were repelled in an invafion of Britain, and that Ireland loft a number of her troops in this unfortunate expedition.— Mr. Macpherfon's affertion therefore, that Claudian's account is not confirmed by any other writer, is not true. And it carries no force with it, if it was. Though the account in Claudian had not been confirmed by any one elfe, the facts in Claudian might yet be real. And his own teftimony would have been fufficient to authenticate the whole.

But

But Ireland, it is objected, may with a juſt poetical propriety be ſaid to lament the ſlaughter even of the Caledonians, if Ireland was peopled from Caledonia, and if the Iriſh and the Caledonians maintained a friendly intercourſe together. If both theſe facts were true, one of which Mr. Macpherſon has vainly attempted to prove before, and the other he now ſuppoſes only; and even if Claudian was acquainted with both; ſuch an introduction of Ireland, as Claudian here makes of Ierne, would certainly be abſurd. It would be abſurd in its own nature, as poetry is not to point at diſtant and generally unknown relations in its perſonifications, but only the near and the known. The former would give ſuch an obſcurity to the beſt imagery of hiſtorical poetry, as would totally prevent its effect. And, if we allowed ourſelves to interpret an hiſtorical poet in this manner, we might pervert the whole ſyſtem of hiſtory. But it would be peculiarly abſurd in the preſent paſſage. Claudian ſpeaks of three diſtinct nations, the Saxons, the Picts, and the Scots; and by his perſonifications he aſſigns them three diſtinct countries, the Orkneys, where the Saxons appear to have ſettled[1], Thule or Caledonia, and Ierne or Ireland. And ſhall Mr. Macpherſon, for the ſake of gratifying the national prejudice of his countrymen,

---

[1] Nennius, c. 37.

countrymen, confound this obvious diſtinction, and make the Scots of Ierne and the Picts of Thule one and the ſame people, and inhabitants of one and the ſame country? And ſhall the ſlaughtered heaps of the Scots, for which Ierne is repreſented as mourning, be only the ſame with the bleeding Picts of Thule? Criticiſm and Common-ſenſe equally concur to forbid it.

There is, it ſhould be obſerved in juſtice to Claudian and the truth, a ſtriking propriety and preciſion in the expreſſions of this paſſage. Theodoſius fitted out a navy, and attacked the Saxons of the Orkneys. Theodoſius marched with an army, and invaded Caledonia. And the expreſſions carry the greateſt adaptedneſs to theſe two incidents. The Orkneys are actually beſmeared with the gore of the Saxons. And Caledonia is actually bathed in the blood of the Picts. But Ireland was not attacked or invaded. The Iriſh were themſelves invaders. And the language is varied accordingly. The two images, that referred before to actual engagements in the Orkneys and in Caledonia, are now diſmiſſed, and another is adopted which ſpeaks only of the conſequence and effect of the engagement to Ierne, of the ſorrow which the news of the defeat diffuſed among the tribes of Ireland. And ſuch an exactneſs and preciſion as this, ſerves ſtrongly to prove the hiſtorical fidelity of Claudian, amid all his poetical imagery.

P. 113

P. 113—115. "In Claudian's Panegyric on
"Stilicho, there is a paffage which has been
"often tranfcribed with triumph in oppofition
"to the antiquity of the Britifh Scots.

"Me quoque vicinis pereuntem gentibus inquit,
"Munivit Stilicho, totam cum Scottus Iernam
"Movit; et infefto fpumavit remige Tethys.
"Illius effectum curis, ne bella timerem
"Scottica, nec Pictum tremerem, nec littore toto
"Profpicerem dubiis venientem Saxona ventis.

"—There is no neceffity to believe that the
"Poet adhered to hiftorical fact. Virgil, with-
"out any authority, extended the victories of
"Auguftus to nations, whom neither He nor
"his lieutenants ever looked in the face: and
"why fhould not the fame privilege of invention,
"exaggeration, and flattery be allowed to the lau-
"reat of Honorius?"

The point which Mr. Macpherfon has undertaken to prove in this Section is, that this and
the preceding paffage of Claudian have been
mifapplied by the criticks, who affert the Irifh
extraction of the Scots. "The abettors of the
"Hibernian Antiquities," he fays in his entrance
upon this examination of Claudian, "—had re-
"courfe to fome paffages of foreign Writers,
"which

" which *they wrested to their purpose*" (p. 110.). But, instead of proving that the passages are wrested, he " ventures to affirm, that there is " nothing in" the former " passage conclusive" against him, and he begs leave to suppose that the latter is full of " invention, exaggeration, " and flattery." And if this would be as readily granted as it is easily affirmed and supposed, the Gordian knot would be untied at once. But, if it is denied, Mr. Macpherson is just where he was before, and the two passages still bear directly against his Hypothesis.

Mr. Macpherson however argues, that because Virgil did, therefore Claudian might, invent, exaggerate, and flatter. But the two cases are very unlike. What Virgil says was entirely prophetic in its designation, and was a little prophetic in reality. Placing himself many centuries before the reign of Augustus, he predictively delineates the glories of that Emperor. And, as his career of honour was not yet run, Virgil adds imaginary to real victories, and anticipates the conquests which he might afterwards make. But Claudian's situation was widely different. He compliments his Emperor upon facts only that were already performed, and that had recently happened. And if, in a poem so immediately retrospective, he had specified any particular facts that had not happened, his compliment must have been spoiled by his folly, and all the court and all the Empire muſt have been equal witneſſes of his falſehood.

P. 114, 115. "We may ſafely affirm, that "the Tethys of Claudian was rather agitated "into a foam by Saxon than by Hibernian oars. "The Saxons, in the days of Honorius, were "in ſome meaſure a maritime people: Tethys "ſignifies the Ocean: the ſea between Germany "and England has ſome right to that title, but "the channel between Ireland and Caledonia "was never dignified with ſo high a name. This "criticiſm is ſufficient to deſtroy the whole force "of the argument drawn from Claudian."

This formidable argument is ſurely a mere accumulation of impertinences.— The Saxons, even more than a century before the days of Honorius, were not only " in ſome meaſure a "maritime people," but were remarkably expert in the arts of navigation. Such they are well known to have been in the days of Carauſius. And ſuch they continued as late as the days of Sidonius:

> Saxona,—cui pelle ſalum ſulcare Britannum Ludus.

—But the verbal criticiſm here is more obſervable. Mr. Macpherſon has repeatedly ſuppoſed before, that Claudian, even in a retro-
ſpective

spective compliment on a recent and notorious event, transgressed the bounds of reality, and threw in imaginary incidents; and that therefore we could not reason from any, even, of the facts which are recorded by him. And yet here Mr. Macpherson can reason from his use of words only. We are taught before by our author, that " it is idle to search for fact in the Hyper-" boles of poetry." And yet here he himself searches for a fact in some lines, which he himself supposes to be so hyperbolical, as to be full of " invention, exaggeration, and flattery ;" and even searches for it in a criticism upon a single word! If Claudian looks unfriendly upon Mr. Macpherson's Hypothesis, even his particular and recent incidents are all hyperbole and fancy. But if Claudian can be brought to cast the coldest look of favour upon it, even his language, even a word confessedly poetical, is neither hyperbolical nor poetical any more.—So far for consistency: now for propriety. Tethys, it is said, signifies Ocean, a name by which the channel between Ireland and Caledonia was never dignified. And this criticism, we are triumphantly told, " is sufficient to destroy the whole force of " the argument drawn from Claudian." But, unhappily for the author, the fact is as untrue as the criticism is trifling. The channel between Ireland and Caledonia is expresly called the Ocean by Ptolemy. Αριθμης πλευρας περιγραφη,

ης υπερκεῖται ΩΚΕΑΝΟΣ καλυμενΘ- ΔυκαλεδονιΘ-.
And to shew what he means by the northern side of Britain, to the North of which lay the Deucaledonian Ocean, Ptolemy begins with the Novantum Promontorium or Mull of Galloway in his progress to the North, ranges up the coast to Faro Head as the northern side of the island, and places the Deucaledonian Ocean along it.

P. 115. " It appears not from history that
" the Scots ever infested the Roman division of
" Britain by sea: Constantine appointed an of-
" ficer called Comes Littoris Saxonici, to take
" the charge of that part of the coast of the
" Province, which was most exposed to the pira-
" tical depredations of the Saxons; but of a
" Comes Littoris Scottici or Hibernici we have
" never heard."

This is a very feeble argument, I think, and very feebly pointed. It begins with a positive assertion, which is not true. And it ends with an inference of reason, which is not just. Though we have heard of a Comes Littoris Saxonici, and have never heard of a Comes Littoris Hibernici, yet it does not thence follow, that the Irish did never invade the shores of Britain. We might not have heard of the one Comes, and yet might have heard of the other. And the Saxon ravages

rages in Britain might be a long repetition of invasions, and therefore occasion the appointment of a particular officer to guard against them; while the Irish might be only a few descents, and would therefore occasion no such appointment. And this appears to have been actually the case. The Irish actually " infested the Ro-" man division of Britain by sea." But they infested it only twice with any considerable armament; once in the days of Theodosius the Elder, and again in the time of Stilicho. And the latter invasion extended even along the whole western shore of the Province, from Lancashire to the Lands End [1].

P. 115, 116. " If the province of Valentia
" comprehended the country between the Walls,
" why did not the Hibernian Scots land every
" other season in Galloway? How came not the
" Irish rovers to attempt a descent in either of
" the divisions of Wales or in Cumberland?
" Was not the coast of Lancashire almost as
" near to the isle of Man, which, according to
" Orosius, was possessed by Scottish tribes, as
" any part of the continent of Caledonia was

---

[1] History of Manchester, p. 458—460.—In supposing therefore the invasion in the days of Stilicho to have been the first, p. 458, I was led by probability, but forgot a fact.

" to

" to Ireland? Why, in the name of wonder,
" was a bullwark of turf and stone a better
" security againſt the Iriſh Scots than againſt
" the Saxons of Friezeland or Holland, as both
" were tranſmarine nations with reſpect to the
" Province? Why did the Iriſh, with a peculiar
" abſurdity, land always on the wrong ſide of
" the Roman Walls, which they muſt have ſcaled
" or deſtroyed before they could penetrate into
" the Province? It is impoſſible to believe that
" all their expeditions could have been ſo ill
" concerted; and this conſideration alone is ſuf-
" ficient to demonſtrate, that the Scots, whom
" the Roman writers ſo often mention, were inha-
" bitants of Caledonia. Walls were conſtructed
" and legions employed to defend the Province
" from their incurſions, but fleets were never
" fitted out to intercept or deſtroy them at
" ſea¹."

The author has here confounded himſelf, by not attending to the very plain diſtinction, betwixt the Scots that came directly from Ireland to invade the Province, and the Scots that were previouſly ſettled in Caledonia. The bullwarks of turf and ſtone were never raiſed againſt the former, any more than againſt the Saxons. And the Iriſh expeditions were not ſo ill concerted, as Mr. Macpherſon ſuppoſes them, on the common

¹ So Sir George Mackenzie argues, more confinedly, in p. 377.

ſyſtem,

THE BRITONS ASSERTED. 199

fyſtem, to have been. They generally invaded the Province from their ſettlement in Argyle, and were accompanied by the Picts. But they twice made a grand invaſion of it directly from Ireland. And this is a full anſwer to this ſeries of Queſtions, why the Scots of Ireland did not land in ſome of the countries to the South of the Walls. They did. In the days of Stilicho particularly, leaving " the country between the " Walls" to be ravaged by their brethren of Argyle and the Picts, they invaded the provinces that were inacceſſible to them, landed in both " of the diviſions of Wales," and now for the firſt time poſſeſſed themſelves of " the iſle of " Man." This is related to us by Nennius in theſe two paſſages. Mailcunius magnus Rex apud Britones regebat, id eſt, in regione Guenedotiæ, quia atavus illius Cunedag cum filiis ſuis—Scotos cum ingentiſſimâ clade expulerat ab iſtis regionibus, et nunquam reverſi fuerunt iterum ad habitandum [1].—Builc autem tenuit Euboniam inſulam cum ſuis [the iſle of Man, ſee c. 2.]; filii autem Vethan obtinuerunt regionem Dimectorum, ubi civitas eſt quæ vocatur Mineu [Menevia or St. Davids]; et in aliis regionibus ſe dilataverunt, i. e. Guiher Cet Guely [to Caer Kidwelly in Caermarthenſhire], donec expulſi ſunt a Cunedâ et a filiis ejus ab omnibus regioni-

[1] C. 64.

bus Britannicis[1]. Here we fee the Scots actually landing in the fouthern divifion of Britain, actually making conquefts in North and South Wales, and actually repelled from both with great flaughter.

Nor were they only beaten from the land. A fleet was " fitted out to deftroy them at fea." This appears plainly from a paffage of Claudian, which Mr. Macpherfon himfelf has quoted in a Note to p. 112—113. It is there faid of Theodofius the Elder, that

   Scottum—vago mucrone fecutus,
Fregit Hyperboreas remis audacibus undas.

Here Mr. Macpherfon himfelf acknowledges, that Theodofius " purfues the Scots fword in hand into the Hyperborean Ocean." A navy was fitted out by Theodofius to deftroy the fleet of Irifh and Saxon veffels, which chaced the former into the northern Ocean, obliged them to retire into the northern ports of Ireland, and then attacked and deftroyed the latter at the Orkneys[2]. And the fea to the North of Ireland is exprefsly denominated the Hyperborean Ocean by Ptolemy.

[1] C. S.   [2] See Latinus and Claudian before.

Mr. Macpherson here gives over his *critical remarks* and *conclusive arguments,* as he calls them, against the customary application of these passages in Claudian. And what has he said against it? That Claudian has perhaps invented and exaggerated facts; that he uses however no exaggerated language; that therefore his Tethys or Ocean cannot signify the channel betwixt Ireland and Caledonia, when the channel is expressly called Ocean by Ptolemy; and that the Scots never landed to the South of the Walls, never infested the southern division of Britain by sea, and were never attacked or pursued at sea by the Romans, when the Scots actually invaded the Provinces by sea in the days of Theodosius, actually landed in North and South Wales, and ravaged all the western shore of Britain, in the days of Stilicho, and were actually pursued by the Roman navy of Theodosius to the North of Ireland.

V.

V.

MR. Macpherson having deprived the opposite fystem, as he imagines, of every support from Claudian; he proceeds to examine the paffages of other writers that have been employed in the fame fervice.

P. 116. "If Orofius, a Spanifh prieft, found the Scots in Ireland about the beginning of the fifth age, Marcellinus met with them in Britain about the middle of the third."

This is all that is faid againft the teftimony of Orofius. And it is evidently nothing. Mr. Macpherson has undertaken to fhew, that thefe paffages of foreign writers are *wrefted* from their natural fignification, when they are applied to prove the Irifh derivation of the Scots of Britain (fee p. 110.). But the authority of Orofius has been cited only to prove, that all the inhabitants of Ireland, from one end of the ifle to another, were denominated Scots. And his words fully evince it: Hibernia infula — a Scotorum gentibus

bus colitur¹. In oppofition to this, Mr. Macpherfon alledges only, that there were Scots in Britain more than 150 years before. This may be true, and the other not be falfe. And hiftory actually fhews it, Orofius and other hiftorians declaring the Irifh to have been all denominated Scots in the fourth and fifth ages, and Bede and others afferting a party of thefe Scots to have migrated into Caledonia. Orofius therefore ftill adheres to the caufe in which he has been fo long engaged. He fhews Ireland to have been the general refidence of the Scottifh tribes, when there was only a fingle nation of them in Caledonia. And Bede and others evince the migration of this from thofe.—Nor did Marcellinus meet with the Scots in Britain about the middle of the *third* century. He firft mentions them after the middle of the *fourth*, and under the year 360².

P. 116—118. " Ifidore of Seville, who flou-
" rifhed in the feventh age, fays, that in his
" time, Ireland was indifcriminately called Scot-
" tia and Hibernia —. Ifidore is not the firft
" learned prelate who gave to Ireland the name
" of Scottia; a bifhop of Canterbury, about the

¹ P. 28, Havercamp.   ² L. xx. c. 1.

" year

" year 605, bestowed upon that island the same
" appellation. We shall not dispute with the
" Irish that their country received the name of
" Scottia some centuries before it was appropri-
" ated to Caledonia. But no argument can arise
" in favour of their superior antiquity from that
" priority. A colony of the antient Grecians
" possessed themselves of a district of the Lesser
" Asia, which afterwards obtained the name of
" Ionia. That colony, and their ancestors in
" Greece, for a series of ages, were called Ioni-
" ans, but their territories in Europe never
" possessed the appellation of Ionia; and from
" that circumstance, will any man conclude, that
" the Ionians of Ephesus and Miletus were more
" antient than those of Attica?"

If Ireland " received the name of Scottia some
" centuries before it was appropriated to Cale-
" donia," as Mr. Macpherson acknowledges,
then the conclusion surely lies very fair and probable, that Ireland was the seat of the Scots some
centuries before Caledonia. And, even if any one
instance could be produced to the contrary, such a
single and solitary incident could not take away the
general tendency of the argument. But no such
instance is here produced. And Mr. Macpherson's parallel is by no means exact. It wants two
essential points of coincidence.

. The

The author's *infinuated* hypothefis here, for he has not ventured to *affirm* it, is this, That the Scots were originally natives of Caledonia, that they firft peopled Ireland, that they there retained their original appellation of Scots, and that they appear bearing the name fome centuries before the Caledonians[1]. This hypothefis indeed is very wild, as it fuppofes the colonifts to retain a name which their anceftors never appear to have borne, and as it makes the children to have been known by their parental appellation fome centuries before the parent herfelf. And the parallel is to be adapted to this. But it is very different. The natives of Attica were denominated Iones, before they fettled a colony in the Leffer Afia: but Mr. Macpherfon has not fhewn, or attempted to fhew, the Caledonians to have been called Scots, before their fuppofed migration into Ireland. The Attic colonifts natu-

---

[1] So Sir George Mackenzie in p. 387 intimates, that the name of Scot belonged to the Caledonians before the Irifh, and was probably communicated by the Caledonians to the Irifh. Dr. Mackenzie alfo in the preface to his Lives of Scots Writers, p. 2—8, attempts to prove Ireland to have been originally peopled by the Caledonians under the name of Scots. And Abercromby fays, p. 2, vol. i, that Dr. Mackenzie bids very fair to prove, that there are greater prefumptions for believing the Scots of Ireland to have come from the Scots in North-Britain, than that the Scots in North-Britain were derived from the Scots in Ireland.

rally

rally settled in Asia under the denomination of their ancestors, and even retained the name when their ancestors had resigned it for another: but, as the Caledonians appear not to have originally possessed the appellation of Scots, so they actually obtained it some centuries after the Irish. These are the two essential points upon which the parallel was to run. But it grossly fails in both. And Mr. Macpherson himself acknowledges it to fail, allowing " the colony and their ancestors in " Greece, for a series of ages," to have been " called Ionians," and yet acknowledging " the " country of the Irish to have received the name " of Scottia some centuries before it was appro- " priated to Caledonia."

This argument therefore is of no moment. And the use that has been made of Isidore's authority stands unimpeached. But the author has made one or two mistakes in this argument, which it may be proper to rectify.

Mr. Macpherson argues, not upon the national appellation of Scoti or Scots, but upon the territorial denomination of Scotia, as if the latter was different from the former, and as if his argument derived a greater weight from this direction of it. " Isidore — says that — Ireland was indiscrimi- " nately called Scottia and Hibernia.—We shall " not dispute with the Irish that their country " received the name of Scottia some centuries,

" before

" before it was appropriated to Caledonia. But
" — a colony of the antient Grecians possessed
" themselves of a district of Lesser Asia, which
" afterwards obtained the name of Ionia. That
" colony, and their ancestors in Greece, for a
" series of ages, were called Ionians, but their
" territories in Europe never possessed the appel-
" lation of Ionia." This is surely a very strange
direction of the argument. If that colony and
their ancestors in Greece were called Ionians,
their territories both in Europe and in Asia must
have possessed the appellation of Ionia. And the
territorial denomination must have commenced
together with the national in both. Isidore accordingly, who mentions the territorial name of
Scotia, mentions also the national apppellation of
Scoti. Coinciding exactly in his words with Orosius above, Isidore, even as quoted by Mr. Macpherson himself, says: Scottia eadem & Hibernia — ; Scottia autem quod ab Scotorum gentibus colitur.

And Mr. Macpherson has forgotten in the
course of his reply to each single authority, that
the notions which he combats do not rely upon
the credit of any of these historians, separately taken, but upon the united force and collective import of all. If Orosius, Isidore, and
others assure us, that Ireland was inhabited by
the Scots in their time, and that it was therefore
denominated

denominated Scotia as well as Hibernia; this forms a ftrongly prefumptive argument, that Ireland was the primary and general feat of the Scots for ages before. But when Bede and others inform us, that Ireland was the original country of the Scots, and that the few Scots, who lived in a narrow confined corner of Caledonia, paffed over from Ireland to fettle there; this reflects a luftre back upon the former affertion, and what before was only prefumptive now becomes certain. And all unite to form thefe important truths, That the Irifh firft bore the appellation of Scots, and firft communicated it to their own country; that they afterwards fettled in Caledonia, and gradually extended their own name over it; and that at laft, as in the cafe of the Ionians above, the colony retained the primæval appellation of their anceftors, when the parent had loft it.

P. 121—128. Mr. Macpherfon having fairly fhewn in p. 118—120, that Gildas's authority is not in reality againft his fcheme; he once more returns to Bede, as he finds his teftimony once more pofitively againft him. And, as before he endeavoured to fet afide his affertions from his uncertainty concerning the reafons of the facts afferted,

asserted, &c., so here he attempts to overthrow his authority by pointing out several mistakes in him.

P. 121, 122. "Whether the Irish Scots ob-
"tained settlements of the Picts by force or fa-
"vour was a point which Bede could not deter-
"mine. He was however informed that they
"were called Dalreudini, from their illustrious
"leader Reuda, and from the Galic word *Deal*,
"which, according to the venerable writer,
"signified a portion or division of a country.
"(—It is to be observed that *Deal* does not sig-
"nify a portion or division)."

This, the first argument against Bede, has been equally urged with another view by Dr. Macpherson in the Critical Dissertations[1]. But, even if it be just, it is of no weight against the authority of Bede. He might be a faithful historian, and yet a very indifferent linguist. He might be very authentic in his account of the Irish migration into Caledonia, and yet be mistaken in his interpretation of an Irish or Caledonian word. What, however, shall we say to these criticks in

[1] P. 53.

the Gallic language, if, after all, they are mistaken and Bede is right. We have seen several reasons before to apprehend, that these gentlemen, who set themselves up as peculiarly qualified to write the antient history of our island, because of their critical acquaintance with its antient language, are but imperfectly acquainted with it. And we have seen them particularly speaking before of the British language, from the view merely of a part of it, and from the knowledge only of one of its dialects. And we see them both more ridiculously speaking here, from a view merely of a part of a part, and from a knowledge only of half a dialect, from an acquaintance with the Irish or Erse, as it is spoken only in the Highlands of Scotland. For in the Erse of Ireland Deal or Dal does signify a portion or division. Bede's assertion, that it so signified in his time, would certainly be a strong presumption that it did, even if it had lost that meaning now. But it has not lost it. The word and its derivatives run through the whole Irish language, and occur in various shapes and forms, all referring to the original idea of division. Deillim and Dealuighim signifies to part or divide, Dailthe and Dealuighte signifies parted or divided, Deilt and Dealachd means a parting or division, and Duil, Dail, and Dal means a division or share. Hence Dail or Dal also signifies in Irish a tribe of people, and the region belonging to it; as in Dal-cais, a name for the tribe of Cormac-cais, and in Dal-araidhe, Dal-fiatach, and Dal-riada, the names of three large territories in Ulster. And the word is not confined to the Irish language. It occurs equally in the Welsh of Howel Dha and in the English of the present day, in the Diler or divider of that great Legiflator, and in the Saxon-British Dealer, To Deal, A Deal, and A Dole, amongst ourselves. The word is so far from not being British, that it appears uncommonly diffused through the British language; forming a large variety of words in the Irish, remaining in the Welsh of the tenth century, and continuing in some of the most familiar words amongst ourselves at present. And how grossly mistaken are both Mr. Macpherson and his friend and fellow-labourer, even in their own province of Celtic etymology!

P. 122. " It is remarkable, that not one
" English or Scottish antiquary ever implicitly
" adopted every part of the Anglo-Saxon's system.
" The Picts and Scots, according to him, as sepa-
" rate nations, and from very different origins,
" possessed North Britain before the commence-
" ment of the Christian æra. Camden, Usher,
" the two Lloyds, Stillingfleet, Innes, and many
" more,

"more, rejected some one part or other, and some the whole of Bede's account of the Southern Britons; but all these learned men received without examination his system of the Hibernian extraction of the British Scots."

This argument is very trifling And Bede's account, of the derivation of the Southern Britons, may be justly rejected either in part or in whole; and yet his account of the extraction of the Scots may be depended upon. The settlement of the former in the island, was long before the existence of records. But the settlement of the latter was within the period of history. For the Scots are not fixed in North-Britain by Bede "before the commencement of the Christian æra." In tracing the origin of the five several nations that were then settled in Britain, Bede begins with the Britons, proceeds to the Picts, and, to give the large account of the Romans and the Saxons in one entire and unbroken series, immediately passes to the Scots, and then enters upon the Romans. And Bede gives us the origin of the Britons, the Picts, and the Scots, in a manner that exactly corresponds with this idea, and that particularly and strikingly distinguishes the antiquity and the recentness of their respective settlements in Britain. Concerning the migration of the Britons and Picts into this island, he expressly speaks with a dubious reference to popular opinions

opinions and traditionary history. But of the migration of the Scots he speaks peremptorily and positively, as peremptorily as he does of the Roman invasion of the island, and as positively as he does of the Saxon settlement upon it. In primis — hæc insula Britones solùm — incolas habuit, qui de tractu Armoricano, *ut fertur*, Britanniam advecti. — Contigit gentem Pictorum de Scythiâ, *ut perhibent*, — Oceanum ingressam, &c. Procedente autem tempore Britannia, post Brittones et Pictos, tertiam Scottorum nationem in Pictorum parte recepit, qui, duce Reudâ de Hiberniâ progressi, vel amicitiâ vel ferro sibimet inter eos sedes quas hactenus habent vindicarunt —. Hibernia propriè patria Scottorum est: ab hâc egressi, ut diximus, tertiam in Britanniâ Brittonibus et Pictis gentem addiderunt [1].

P. 122, 123. " Where we have an oppor-
" tunity to examine Bede's account by the
" criterion of collateral history, we find that he
" has committed a very essential mistake. The
" Southern Britons were so far from deriving
" their blood from the inhabitants of Armorica,
" that, on the contrary, the Armoricans had
" transmigrated from Britain not many ages be-

[1] L. i. c. 1.

" fore

"fore Bede's own time. If Bede therefore was
"in an error with refpect to the origin of a
"people, whofe hiftory, on account of their
"connection with the Romans, was known, it
"is much more probable that he knew nothing
"certain concerning the antiquities of a nation,
"who had not among them the means of pre-
"ferving, with any certainty, the memory of
"events."

This is the third argument againft Bede. And it is, I think, of as little avail as the other two.—Bede has committed no miftake, even upon Mr. Macpherfon's own ftate of the cafe. He derives the original Britons from Armorica: but he derives them very dubioufly. In primis, fays he, hæc infula Britones folûm, a quibus nomen accepit, incolas habuit, qui de tractu Armoricano, *ut fertur*, Britanniam advecti [1]. And his derivation of the original Britons from Armorica, even if pofitively afferted, does not fuperfede, as Mr. Macpherfon imagines, the re-migration of Britons into Armorica afterwards, becaufe it is not contrary to it.

The name of Armorica feems, from the fhifting application of it by antient authors, and from the full import of the word, which fignifies the people upon the fea, to have once extended

[1] Lib. i. c. i.

along

along the whole compass of the Gallic coast from the Bay of Biscay to the Rhine. In the days of Cæsar it comprized a variety of states in Western Gaul [1]. In the days of Pliny it reached from the Pyrenees to the Garonne [2]. And in the days of Sidonius Apollinaris it was carried much farther to the North-East, and included, and even seems to have been restricted to, the compass of the present Bretagne [3]. In this general acceptation of the word, the Britons were certainly derived from Armorica. And at the eastern point of the Gallic coast, and directly opposite to the great Angle of Kent, even Bede places the Morini, a name exactly the same as Ar-Mor-ic-i, and seemingly the continuation of it [4].

Whether the Britons ever re-migrated into France, and fixed the appellation of Britanni upon the continent, has been much disputed. But, I think, it may be satisfactorily settled. That they actually transmigrated, is evident from history. They passed into Gaul under the conduct of Maximus, and settled afterwards in Armorica, as is asserted by Llomarch Hen and by Nennius [5]. And they settled in Gaul upon the first invasion of the Saxons, as is asserted by Gildas, by Bede, and by Eginhard [6]. But in

[1] P. 108.   [2] L. iv. c. 17.   [3] Carte, V. I. p. 7. a note.   [4] L. i. c. 1.   [5] Carte, V. I. p. 169. a note; and Nennius, c. 23.   [6] Gildas, c. 25. alii transf-

both these migrations they did not establish themselves in Bretagne only. The greatest number passed over under Maximus[1]; and these were dispersed in the many regions that extend a stagno quod est super verticem Montis Jovis usque ad civitatem quæ vocatur Cantguic, from the great St. Bernard in Piedmont to Cantavic in Picardy, and from Picardy to the western coast of France[2]. And the refugees, that were driven away by the Saxon invasion, appear to have equally dispersed themselves into different parts of the continent, transmarinas regiones petivere. In both expeditions however, a body of them seems certainly to have planted themselves in the present Bretagne[3]. But they never fixed the name of Britanni on the continent. It was there ages before either migration. Dionysius the Geographer, and Pliny the Naturalist, both speak of the Britanni, as the name of a tribe on the borders of Picardy and Flanders[4]. And Britannia, the capital of the tribe assuredly, was one of the most celebrated cities in Gaul, as early as the days of Hannibal[5]. Armorica is

---

marinas petebant regiones, Bede, l. i. c. 15. the same, and Eginhard in Ann. Franc. Usher, p. 226. edit. 1687.

[1] Gildas, c. 11. ingenti juventute.   [2] Nennius, c. 23. The common copies read Tantguic, but the Cotton M. S. Cantguic. And for Cantavic see Carte, V. I. p. 25. a note. [3] Carte, V. I. p. 259. from Llomarch, and the writers in Usher, p. 226.   [4] Carte, p. 5.   [5] Ibid. a note.

called

called Britannia by Sulpicius Severus, at a time when it appears to have been equally called Armorica. And as Sulpicius wrote within 10 years only after the expedition of Maximus, so he recites the name without any note of its novelty, and even in speaking of the times antecedent to that expedition [1]. And in the same manner, within 12 years only from the first possible migration of the islanders in consequence of the Saxon invasion, and within 4 only after the Saxons had made themselves masters of a single county [2], even in the year 461, and even in the public acts of a Synod, the Prelate of Armorica subscribes himself, without hesitation, without explanation, Mansuetus Bishop of the Britons [3]. Each argument separately proves, and the actual and exact concurrence of both gives a great additional weight to the proof, that the names of Armorica and Britannia were equally the appellations of the country, long before the forces of

---

[1] Carte, p. 6, 7. a note.   [2] Sax. Chron.

[3] Usher, p. 226.—Mr. Carte has strangely supposed such a number of Britons to have retired from Kent, that Hengist was obliged to bring a body of his countrymen, about 300,000, from Germany to supply their place (V. I. p. 195.).—And Dr. Borlase, still more strangely, supposes the Britons to have retired into Armorica " when the Saxons had conquered " the greatest part of the island" (P. 39. edit. 2d.), though the name of the Britons occurs in Armorica so many years before that period.

Maximus

Maximus or the refugees of Kent could have settled in it. It is ridiculous to suppose, that they settled there in any considerable numbers. No numbers could have imposed their own appellation upon the country, without an absolute conquest of the natives. And as, in the circumstances of both the colonies, a conquest of Armorica was absolutely impracticable, so the name of Britain appears the well-known, the acknowledged, the customary appellation of Armorica, within 10 years only after the first migration, and even within 4 only after the last.

The name of Britons, then, was the antient and equal appellation of the Armoricans, as in the History of Manchester I have shewn the names of Morini and Rhemi to have been for the Durotriges and Bibroces; was taken up in the later ages of the Empire, and at last superseded the other. And these appellations of Britons for the Celtæ of Armorica, of Picardy, or of Flanders, were all evidently occasioned by the same principles of distinction, that planted Pict-on-es in France and Pict-i in Scotland, and that settled Brigantes equally on the continent and in the island. The principle which stamped the appellation of Britanni, Brigantes, or the separated People, upon the Gauls that had crossed the channel into Albion, as naturally operated to give the same name to the Gauls which were separated from the rest by much slighter barriers,

riers, by a few hills of the Alps, or by a couple of currents. And we see the case strongly exemplified in the equivalent word Vict or Pict, applied, as I have shewn in the History of Manchester, to those Britons who were strikingly distinguished from the rest by lying without the pale of the Roman Province, and equally applied to the Pictones in Gaul, who were only divided from the rest by rivers, and to the Vect-urion-es in Caledonia, who were only separated from the rest by mountains [*].

[*] History of Manchester, p. 415—417. The word is also applied, in Vectis, Ictis, or Wight, to a land that was merely peninsular, and that was only insulated at the tide of flood; and, in Portus Ictius or Wit-sand, merely to such an opening or division in the land as formed an harbour: And it therefore stands for an island in the Welsh Uigt (Baxter on Vectis) and the Saxon-Welsh Ight, and for a cove or creek in the Cornish Ic or Ict, at present. How wrong then are Mr. Carte and Dr. Borlase; the one, in drawing an argument for the conjunction of Britain to Gaul from the name of the Promontorium Ictium, because the name signifies separation (p. 3.); and the other, for transferring the Ictis of Diodorus from the isle of Wight to Cornwall, because the name signifies a Cove in Cornish (Borlase's Scilly). The harbour must have given name to the Promontory. And Ict must have signified an harbour equally in the Gallic and in the British.—And so we have Brixia, now Brescia, in the Gallic part of Italy, as the Britons of France now call themselves Brez, and as Brix signifies a rupture or division at present. And so Bruges in Flanders, Bretten the antient name of Mons in Hainault, &c. (See Carte, p. 6. and 10.).

Bede

Bede then has not committed, as Mr. Macpherson asserts, " a very essential mistake " here. He has committed none at all. He deduces the original Britons from Armorica, perhaps extending that name along the whole coast of France, and being then certainly right in his deduction. One of his reasons was the continuing appellation of Britons in Gaul, perhaps in Flanders or Picardy, and certainly in Bretagne. And the other was the general tradition of the times. But he gives us all with a strong note of diffidence, referring us to his single authority, and declaring that to be only the popular opinion. By his ascribing the name of the Insular to the Continental Britons, he plainly shews, that he considered the name as existing in Gaul, many ages before the invasion of the Saxons or the rebellion of Maximus. And we have seen sufficiently above, that the name was actually prior to both.

I have entered the more fully into this argument, because it might seem to carry some degree of force with it. And I was desirous to ascertain the triflingness of the British migrations into Gaul, which had been considerably heightened, to point out the existence of the name of Britons there before them, and to lay open the grounds and reasons of the name consistently with the etymology of Britain before. Mr. Carte, pursuing the steps of Bede, had endeavoured to

derive

derive the name of our own Britons from the remaining appellation on the continent, but had not afferted the meaning of either. And he had even, contradictorily, derived the name of Bretagne from the tranfplanted Britons of this ifland [1]. And I was willing, in anfwer equally to Mr. Macpherfon and Mr. Carte, to vindicate the real hiftory, if I could, and to reduce it into a regular confiftency.

P. 123. " From the political and religious
" prejudices which prevailed, in the days of Bede,
" between the Britifh Scots and the Saxons, we
" may conclude that the venerable writer had
" very little converfation with the antiquaries or
" fenachies of the former nation. Had he even
" confulted them, very little light could be de-
" rived from them in an age of ignorance, cre-
" dulity, and barbarifm. Bede, on the other
" hand, entertained a friendly partiality for the
" Scots of Ireland.—Their benevolence and hof-
" pitality to the Saxon Students, who flocked
" into their country, recommended them, in a
" very high degree, to the venerable Anglo-Saxon
" (Bede Hift. lib. iv. c. 26.). The good man,
" we may take it for granted, embraced every
" opportunity of converfing with thofe Hibernian

[1] Carte, p. 5, 6. and 194, 195. V. I.

" miffionaries

"missionaries and pilgrims who came over in
"swarms into Britain, in those days of conver-
"sion and religious pilgrimage. From them he
"borrowed all that genealogical erudition which
"he displays in the beginning of his Ecclesiastical
"History [1]."

This is the fourth argument against Bede. And it is obviously all founded upon guesses, assumptions without reason, and conclusions without premisses.—It is presumed, that Bede had very little conversation with the Caledonians, and a great deal with the Irish. It is therefore inferred, that he derived his account of the Scots, not from the former, but from the latter. And it is again inferred, that his accounts are therefore wrong. Such is the nature of the present argument. And the presumption and the inferences are all equally unjust.

A very great intimacy had commenced betwixt the Northumbrians and the Caledonians, from the kind refuge which the sons of Ethelfrid had found among them, after the death of their father in 617. And a considerable correspondence was carried on between them to the days of Bede. Filii — regis Ædilfridi, says Bede, — cum magnâ nobilium juventute apud Scottos sive Pictos exulabant, ibique ad Scottorum doctrinam catechizati

[1] So the Prefacer to Dr. Macpherson, p. vi and xiii.

sunt.

funt¹. And a few years afterward Ofwald the king, and a number of adherents with him, were received with equal hofpitality, and were equally baptized, among the Scots: inter quos exulans Ipfe Baptifmatis facramenta, cum his qui fecum erant militibus, confecutus erat². At Ofwald's departure from the country, he appears to have made himfelf a perfect mafter of the Scotch language: tam longo exilii fui tempore linguam Scottorum jam plenè didicerat³. And, upon his recovery of Northumbria from Cadwallaun, he fent and procured a bifhop and various other teachers from the Country, and the Northumbrians became the pupils and difciples of the Scots: mifit ad majores natu Scottorum—, petens ut fibi mitteretur antiftes —; accepit — pontificem Aidanum — ; exin cœpere plures per dies de Scottorum regione venire Britanniam, atque illis Anglorum provinciis quibus regnavit rex Ofuald — verbum fidei prædicare —; imbuebantur præceptoribus Scottis parvuli Anglorum⁴. And this continued the regular ftate of Northumbria for 30 or 40 years together, the three fucceffive bifhops of Northumbria being all Scotch, king Ofwi and bifhop Chad being well acquainted with the Scotch language, and even the foutherly

¹ Bede, l. iii. c. 1.   ² L. iii. c. 3.
³ Ibid.   ⁴ Ibid.

kingdom

kingdom of Mercia being governed at the same period by two succeſſive Scotch biſhops [1]. This continued to the year 664 [2]. And a frequent intercourſe was carried on by the Northumbrians with the Scots and Picts afterwards, even to the death of Bede. This hiſtorian was born within nine years after the termination of the Scottiſh biſhops, and finiſhed his hiſtory in the 59th year of his age and the 731ſt after Chriſt [3]. King Oſwi, who had been educated among the Scots [4], extended his empire over a part of the Picts, and ſubjected his new dominions to the one biſhop of Northumbria [5]. Theſe were afterwards, in 681, formed into a ſeperate dioceſs by king Egfrid [6], and continued ſo to the year 685 [7]. In the year 701 Adamnan, the Abbot of Hii, was ſent on an embaſſy by the Scots to Alfrid king of Northumbria, reſided ſome time in the country, and was converted by the Northumbrian ſcholars to the Saxon mode of obſerving Eaſter [8]. In 710 the monarch of the Picts ſent embaſſadors to Ceolfrid, the Abbot of Bede's own monaſtery, who had converſed with Adamnan before [9], and with whom Bede was then, and had been for

---

[1] L. iii. c. 21, 24, and 25.   [2] C. 26.
[3] P. 795, Smith.   [4] L. iii. c. 25 and 29.
[5] L. iv. c. 3.   [6] L. iv. c. 12.
[7] L. iv. c. 26.   [8] L. v. c. 15.
[9] P. 215.

very

very many years, resident in the monastery; requesting proper information from him concerning the observance of Easter[1]. The information was given, and all the Picts conformed to the Saxon mode[2]. And in 716 Egbert, a Northumbrian clergyman, went among the Scots, resided 13 years with them, and converted numbers of them to the same mode[3]. From this particular detail of facts it appears plainly, that Bede had sufficient opportunities of conversing with the Caledonians and Caledonian Scots, and of knowing the origin of the latter from the united accounts of both. The political and religious prejudices of the Saxons are shewn to have been pretty equal against the Caledonians and the Irish. And the Northumbrians appear to have had a much greater intercourse with their neighbours of Caledonia, than with the natives of Ireland. The political prejudices of the Saxons against the former did not, as Mr. Macpherson imagines, make the communication between them small, but naturally operated to increase it by the reduction of a large extent of Caledonia, and actually united a very considerable body of the Picts for many years to Northumbria. And the religious prejudices of the Saxons against the

---

[1] L. v. c. 21.   [2] Ibid.
[3] L. v. c. 22. and p. 33.

Caledonians, which Mr. Macpherson alledges as the preventive cause of much communication betwixt them, prevented not the Saxon kings and the Saxon nobles, we see, from being educated among the Scots, or from inviting Scottish bishops and Scottish teachers into Northumbria, before the days of Bede, and were actually the occasion of visits, conferences, and embassies between them to the period of his writing. For more than a century before it, the Northumbrians had been particularly conversant with the Picts and Scots. And, at it, there were no religious and political prejudices subsisting at all betwixt them. Both the Picts and the Scots were then in a state of peace and friendliness with the Northumbrians. A great part of the Scots had been then converted by Saxon preachers to the Saxon observance of Easter. And the whole body of the Picts had then adopted the ceremonial of Northumbria[1].

Thus is the main point of Mr. Macpherson's argument refuted by positive authority. And such is the unhappy construction of this and of many of Mr. Macpherson's arguments, that it is not only an assertion without proof, that it is not only actually false in itself, but that, if true, it would prove nothing. It is not of the least mo-

[1] L. v. c. 23, &c.

ment to the authenticity of the fact, whether Bede derived his knowledge of it from the Scots of Ireland or the Scots of Caledonia. Either muſt have been a ſufficient and competent authority for the fact. And, even according to Mr. Macpherſon's own account in this very extract, the Iriſh Scots muſt have been the beſt hiſtorians, as the Caledonian were then in a ſtate of " ignorance, " credulity, and barbariſm," and as Ireland was the ſeat of learning even to the Engliſh, and the " Saxon ſtudents *flocked* into the country."

P. 124. Having triflingly obſerved, that " the " ſudden tranſition which Bede makes from the " tale of Reuda to a panegyric on Ireland," and afterwards concluding with a new declaration of the ſame tale, furniſhes a ſtrong preſumption that he derived his information from the Iriſh ; Mr. Macpherſon proceeds thus — " It is apparent " from another circumſtance, that Bede borrow- " ed his account of the Scots from the Iriſh. He " calls the inhabitants of Iar-ghael [Argyle] by " the name of Dalreudini, an appellation ut- " terly unknown to the hiſtorians, writers of " chronicles, bards, and ſenachies of Scotland, " though common in the annals of Ireland."

I have already obferved, that it is not of the leaft fignification to the truth and authenticity of the hiftory, whether Bede derived it from the Scots of Ireland or the Scots of Caledonia, and that, even according to Mr. Macpherfon himfelf, the learned Irifh were more likely to give Bede true information concerning an antient incident, than their ignorant and barbarous brethren of Argyle. And the fact and the reafoning here are neither of them true.

Bede afferts the Scots of Caledonia to have been actually denominated Dalreudini in his time: ufque hodie Dalreudini vocantur[1]. This is not a particular, that could have been borrowed from the Irifh annalifts. He fpeaks of a fact notorious and public, and exifting in his own time. It was the popular name of the Scots among the nations around them, in the days of Bede. This therefore is a fact that muft have been known to Bede himfelf. And his affertion is decifive for its exiftence.

P. 125, 126. "To deftroy from another " principle, the tale of Bede and the ftory of " Reuda, it may not be improper to obferve, that

[1] L. i. c. 1.

" the

"the learned Usher found out that a district in
"the county of Antrim, which has for many ages
"been distinguished by the name of *Route*, is
"the Dalriada of the old Irish. Dalriada, says
"the ingenious prelate, derives its name from
"Cairbre-Riada, the son of Conaire, who held
"the sceptre of Ireland in the third century. But
"we may venture to affirm that Usher, in this
"supposition, was very much misled. Rute or
"Reaidh in the old Scottish language signifies
"a Ram, — and — Dalriada literally the val-
"ley of the Ram. Usher quotes a patent which
"is preserved in the Tower of London, wherein
"it appears, that John king of England granted to
"Allan Lord of Galloway the territory of Dal-
"reth and the island of Rachrin, which is situ-
"ated over-against that district. From the sylla-
"bication of the two local names in the patent,
"we may conclude that the etymon we have
"given of Dalriada is perfectly just. Rachrin,
"which may, with great propriety, be reckoned
"an appendage to the *Route*, signifies the Ram's
"promontory in the Irish tongue; and Dalriada
"itself being expressly called the land of Rams,
"in the Irish patent mentioned by the primate
"himself, is a circumstance that is decisive in our
"favour."

This is the sixth argument against the assertion of Bede. And it is obviously no argument at all againſt him. It relates only to Uſher. And it has no more tendency "to deſtroy the tale of "Bede and the ſtory of Reuda," than it has to diſprove the doctrine of gravitation or the theory of the comets. Uſher's etymon of Dalriada may be unjuſt: and yet the account of the Dalreudian colony in Bede would be unimpeached. And, what is ſtill more ſtrange in the formation of this argument, Uſher may have really "found out "that a diſtrict in the county of Antrim, which "has for many ages been diſtinguiſhed by the "name of Route, is the Dalriada of the Iriſh:" and yet his derivation of Dalriada from Cairbre-Riada may be falſe. In the firſt caſe, Mr. Macpherſon's argument is not pointed at all againſt the hiſtorical fact in Bede, though it pretends to deſtroy it. And, in the ſecond, his argument is not levelled at all againſt the geographical fact in Uſher, though it is deſigned to overthrow it.

Having thus eaſily ſhewn the ſtrange incompetency of the argument in general, we ſhall have more leiſure to point out Mr. Macpherſon's other miſtakes in the courſe of it. Theſe are, That the Route in Antrim was ſo called from Rute a Ram; That Dalriada ſignifies literally the valley of the Ram; That Rachrin means the Ram's Promontory; and, That "Dalriada itſelf
                                    "being

" being expresly called the land of Rams, in
" the Irish patent mentioned by the primate
" himself, is a circumstance that is decisive in
" Mr. Macpherson's favour." This last assertion
is an unaccountable mistake. Dalriada is neither
expresly nor implicitly called the land of Rams
in Usher's patent, as mentioned by himself. All
that he says of it is this: Totam—Dalreth sive
Dalrede, cum insulâ Rachlyn vel Rachrin, illi
objacente, Alano de Galway, a Johanne Anglorum Rege & Hiberniæ Domino concessam olim
fuisse, ex archivis Regiis in arce Londinensi asser-
vatis constat (Patent in Dorso ann. 14 R. Johan-
nis, Membran. 3. Num. 1., et ann. 17. Membran. 5. Num. 57); quam utramque nunc
jure possideat hereditario Comes Antrimensis [1].
And, as the circumstance decisive in Mr. Macpherson's favour appears not upon the face
of the Archbishop's account, so Mr. Macpherson's etymons contradict every idea of propriety.—Riada or Reaidhe, we see, is used not
only conjunctively with Dal, as in Dal-riada, but
separately by itself, as in Route. And to denominate any country simply Reaith or Ram, is
an evident absurdity. This overthrows the etymology of both at once. The true derivation
must be one, that will conform itself with propriety to the name of Route, as well as to the
appellation of Dal-riada. And such is Ruta, the

[1] P. 321.

fame in Irish as Route in English, and fignifying in an honourable acceptation a tribe of people; a name, with the greateft propriety applicable to that divifion of Antrim which is denominated Route, to the Dal-reud-ini of Scotland, and to the Dal-reth of Ireland, and importing the tribe and the country of it. — Nor can Rachlyn or Rachrin fignify the Ram's promontory. A Ram is in Irifh, not Rach, but Reaith; and Mr. Macpherfon has already deduced Route and Reaidhe from it. And the other word is not Ryn only, but is equally Lyn, Rachlyn vel Rachrin. This is not a promontory, but an ifland, infula Rachlyn vel Rachrin, and is actually an ifland, and actually denominated Rachlin, at prefent. The name clearly terminating in the word In an ifland, it feems to begin with the Irifh word Rak-ol, and to import the Royal ifland. And hence it is denominated Ric-in-a, Reich-in, or King-ifland, by Ptolemy [1].

P. 127,

[1] Mr. Macpherfon alfo objects in p. 126, That "according to the genius of the Irifh language" Dal-riada, if called from Cairbre-Riada, muft have been, not Dal-Riada, but Dal-Cairbre, becaufe Riada is only a pofterior and fecondary name. But we have feveral inftances to the contrary in the Irifh hiftory, which, however fpurious as facts, are certainly agreeable to the genius of the Irifh language, as Dal-araidhe in Down and Antrim from Fiacha-araidhe, king of Ulfter towards

P. 127, 128. " Usher has ascertained the
" bounds of Dalriada, or the *Route* in Antrim,
" and found its whole extent about 30 miles.
" Were it even certain that Dalriada produced
" more men than any district of the same extent
" in antient Ireland, still it is incredible, that an
" army could be muttered there sufficient to sub-
" due the principality of Iar-ghael [Argyle]."

All the arguments that are founded on a supposition, of the Scotch settling in Caledonia by violence, have been already shewn to be beside the mark. No one, I think, has ever insisted upon the settlement being originally effected by force. And the amicable concurrence of the Caledonian Scots with the Picts in expeditions into the Roman province, within a few years only after their first establishment in Britain, is a full and convincing proof, as I have already remarked, that the one fixed themselves in the country with the entire consent of the other.

wards the middle of the third century, and as Dal-Cais from Cormac-Cais, king of Munster and Leinster in the same century.—Rachryn seems to be equally the true name with Rachlyn, as the islet is called Rechru and Rachrea in Adamnan's Life of Columba (L. i. c. 5. p. 340, and L. ii. c. 41. p. 361, Colgan's Acta Sanctorum Hiberniæ, vol. ii.). And this is Reich-er-y, or Rach-er-ea, the Kingman's island, literally.

THE

The author here difmiffes Bede for the fecond time. And what he has advanced againſt him, Ifidore, and Orofius, are reafonings merely problematical, arguments that have forgot their direction, and proofs that evince nothing; violent affertions without authority, ſtrong depofitions in the face of hiſtory, and etymologies egregiouſly fantaſtical and trifling. This account, I hope, is not too fevere. I give it merely from my own feelings, fenfibly offended as they have been through the whole courfe of this fection. And, while I wiſh to be polite to Mr. Macpherfon, I cannot but feverely condemn the negligence and haſtinefs of the hiſtorian.

VI.

VI.

DISMISSING these semblances of reasons, Mr. Macpherson now advances to what he denominates in the margin his " conclu-" sive arguments." And, here at least, we shall meet with reasonings that may be worthy of the author.

P. 129. " As a concluding argument against
" the Hibernian extraction of the Scots, it may
" not be improper to observe, that the Caledo-
" nians might be called Hibernians, their coun-
" try in general Hibernia, and the western
" division of it Ierna or Yverdhon, without de-
" riving their blood from the Irish. The Saxons
" of England, it is well known, had their Norfolk
" and Suffolk, and the appellation of Southerons
" and Norlands are not hitherto totally extin-
" guished among the Scots [the Scotch Low-
" landers]: the antient Picts, in like manner,
" were divided into two great tribes, the Vectu-
" riones and Deucaledones, the inhabitants of the
" Northern

"Northern and Southern divisions, according to
"the testimony of Marcellinus. (Eo tempore
"Picti in duas gentes divisi, Deucaledonas et
"Vecturiones. Ammian. Marcellin. lib. xxvii.
"Camdenus, vir in patriâ historiâ illustrandâ ac-
"curatissimus, legendum putat Deucaledonios,
"velut sic nominatos ab occiduâ Scotiæ orâ, quâ
"Deucaledonius oceanus irrumpit)."

This, we see, is called "a concluding argu-
"ment" by Mr. Macpherson. And I am sorry
to observe, that it appears upon the very face of
it, it appears even as Mr. Macpherson has stated
it, to amount to no proof, to amount not even
to a presumption, but to rise only to a mere
possibility. "As a concluding argument—, it
"may be proper to observe, that the Caledo-
"nians *might* be called Hibernians &c." Nor is
the argument any other in itself, as it infers,
that the Caledonians *might* be called Hibernians,
because the Saxons had a Norfolk and Suffolk,
the Scots were once divided into Southerons and
Norlands, and the Picts were once broken into
Northern and Southern Vecturiones and Deucaledones. And this is surely the first, merely
possible, argument that was ever advanced against
an historical fact; and is, I hope, the last that
will be denominated a conclusive one.

So far for the argument in general. Let us now examine the particular parts of it. Grofsly inaccurate as it is in the principal point, it cannot be exact in the fubordinate circumftances. And it is not.

Marcellinus does not fay, as he is here quoted, that the Vecturiones and Deucaledones were the northern and fouthern Picts. He makes not the leaft mention of either North or South. And he was unacquainted with the name of De*u*caledones, though Mr. Macpherfon, in direct contradiction to his own Latin note, quotes him as ufing it. Picti in duas gentes divifi, he fays, D*i*calidonas et Vecturiones. The Vecturiones I have fhewn in the Hiftory of Manchefter to be only a fingle tribe, that inhabited a part of Perth and Mar, and all Gawry, Angus, and Merns, between them [1]. And D*y*caledones I have equally fhewn to be the fame word with De*u*caledones in Britifh, and Ammianus's text therefore to need no alteration [2]. Thefe Mr. Camden very juftly fuppofed to be the tribes along the Deucaledonian Ocean of Ptolemy. But their name does not fignify a pofition to the Weft, as Mr. Camden imagined, or a fituation to the North, as Archbifhop Ufher and Mr. Macpherfon fuppofe. Thefe and Baxter interpret Deu the Weft, the North, and the South. But it

[1] P. 10.   [2] P. 423.

plainly

plainly relates to none of them. Du or Deu fignifies Water, as in Du-bana, the river Ban in Ireland, and as in Deu-draeth, or the Sea-beach, the name of feveral places in Wales[1]. And the nations of weftern Caledonia were denominated Deu-caledon or the Maritime Caledonians, as the wefterly tribes of Gaul were named Aremorici or the Gauls of the fhore; as a fingle maritime people in Gaul and in Britain was called Morini and Durotriges, the people of the Sea, or the inhabitants on the Water; and as the Highlanders that live in a line along the fhore of Scotland, in Rofs, Sutherland, and Cathnefs, are fometimes denominated by their interior brethren An-Dua-Ghael, or the Water-Britons, to the prefent moment[2].

From this account it is plain, that the paffage in Ammianus has been hitherto misfunderstood by the criticks. He means not by it, that the great fociety of the Picts was divided into Dicaledones and Vecturiones. The Vecturiones were only a fingle tribe on the Eaft. And the Dicaledones comprehended only a few tribes on the Weft. All the other nations in the Eaft, the North, and the South of Caledonia, according to this interpretation, are thrown out of the number of the Picts, and ranked as different and

---

[1] Hiftory of Manchefter, p. 423. [2] Hiftory of Manchefter, p. 423.

diftinct from them. The author is therefore to be interpreted, not concerning the body of the Picts in general, but of that particular army of them which now ravaged the Province. And this he afferts to have been levied from two divifions of the country, from the long line of the Dicaledonian tribes, which were fituated upon the weftern fhore, and from the fingle nation of the Vecturiones, which was placed upon the eaftern. Eo tempore Picti, in duas gentes divifi, Dicalidonas et Vecturiones, itidemque Attacotti, bellicofa hominum natio, et Scotti, per diverfa vagantes multa populabantur.

Thus unfortunate is Mr. Macpherfon in the commencement of his conclufive reafonings. And thus grofsly miftaken is he, equally in the principal point and the fubordinate circumftances of his firft argument.

P. 129, 130. "If the Picts fpoke the—
" Caledonian language, they muft certainly have
" called the territories of the Scots [in Caledo-
" nia], Iar, Eire, Erin,—words, all of them,
" expreffive of the fituation of the country of
" the Scottifh tribes, in oppofition to the Pictifh
" divifion of Caledonia; if they fpoke the antient
" Britifh, they would have diftinguifhed the
" country of the Scots by the name of Yverdhon,
" or,

"or, as it is pronounced, Yberon or Yveron.
"These names being communicated to the Ro-
"mans by the Britons, or by Pictish prisoners, it
"was natural for them to latinize them into Ierna,
"Iouverna, or Hibernia. In common conver-
"sation, the western Highlands are called by
"those who speak the Galic language IAR, or
"the West; and when the Hebrides are com-
"prehended in that division of Scotland, the Ga-
"lic appellation of Iar-in has been always given
"to the whole. The district of Arre-gathel, or
"rather Iar-ghael, so often mentioned in the
"annals of Ireland and Scotland, as the first
"possessions of the Hibernian colonies in Bri-
"tain, carries in its name a demonstration of
"this position, as well as a decisive argument
"against the antient system of the origin of the
"Scots. Iar-ghael literally signifies the *western
"Gael*, or the Scots, in opposition to the *eastern
"Gael*, or the Picts, who possessed the shore of
"the German Ocean."

This is the second conclusive argument against the Hibernian extraction of the Scots. And I have quoted it in all its extent, that it may not be deprived of any necessary part, but may stand the trial in its full force and power. It consists of these two great particulars; That Iar, Eir, Erin, and Yverdhon or Yberon, are names by which the Picts must have distinguished

the

the Scottish territories in Caledonia, as the western Highlands are to this day popularly denominated Iar by the Highlanders, and, when the Hebrides are included, Iar-in, and are the origin of the Greek and Roman appellations of Ierna, Iuverna, and Hibernia; and that the name of Argyle, Arre-gathel, or rather Iar-ghael, literally signifies the western Gael, and so distinguished the Scots from the Picts, as the Gael of the western from the Gael of the eastern coast. And both of these positions I will examine attentively.

The conclusive argument before, according to Mr. Macpherson's own state of it and the truth, amounted only to a possibility. This assumes the confidence of certainty, and pretends to be decisive. " The Picts—*must certainly* have called &c. " — *a decisive argument* against the antient system " of the origin of the Scots, &c." But the certainty and decisiveness of this is little better than the possibility of that.

The former half of this argument makes the western Highlands of Scotland to be the Ierna, Iuverna, and Hibernia of the antients. And in p. 112—113 we are referred to the present passage, as actually proving the probability at least of the position. But, in opposition to it, we need only reflect upon what Strabo, Cæsar, and Mela, the first authors that mention Ierna, Iuverna, and Hibernia, have said of each. Strabo, the first certain writer who speaks of Ierna, says

says thus of it: εισι δε και αλλαι περι την Βρεττανικην νησοι μικραι· μεγαλη δ'η Ιερνη προς αρκτον παραβεβλημενη, προμηκης μαλλον δε πλοιος εχυσα¹. Mela, the first who speaks of Iuverna, says thus: Supra Britanniam Iuverna est, penè par spatio, sed utrinque æquali tractu littorum oblonga². And Cæsar, the first who mentions Hibernia, says thus: alterum [latus Britanniæ] vergit ad—occidentem solem, quâ ex parte est Hibernia, dimidio minor, ut existimatur, quam Britannia; sed pari spatio transmissus atque ex Galliâ est in Britanniam; in hoc medio cursu est insula quæ appellatur Mona³. And these descriptions will not agree at all with the western Highlands of Scotland. They are not above⁴, or to the West of, Britain, but are

---

¹ Strabo, p. 307.—I quote not Orpheus, because the work attributed to him, or to Orpheus of Crotona (see Usher, p. 378.), is assuredly spurious. And I even quote not Aristotle's treatise De Mundo, though it is quoted as his by Mr. Carte (p. 4. V. l.), and though it is quoted as his, or Theophrastus's, or some person's cotemporary with both, by Usher (p. 378.); for the same reason that I quoted it not before, to prove the name of Briton prior to Mr. Macpherson's Cimbri, because I consider it as the work of a later period, probably, as some criticks have supposed, written about the reign of Augustus.

² L. iii. c. 6.   ³ P. 89.   ⁴ So the western side of Roman Britain was called Britannia Superior or Higher Britain, and the eastern Britannia Inferior or Lower Britain (History of Manchester, p. 59.).—And, as to Strabo's προς Αρκτον, all the western side of Britain from Galloway to the Orkneys was stiled the northern side of it.

actually

actually a part of it. They are not about one half, or nearly the whole, of the compafs of Britain, but are actually a part, and a fmall part, of it. And they are not divided from Britain by a fea as broad as the Gallic, in the middle of which lies the ifle of Man; they are not one of the many ifles that lie about Britain; and they are not a great ifland, whofe two oppofite fides are equal in length, and which is broader than it is long: but they are a narrow tract of country within the ifland of Britain, lie along the eaftern border of that fea in which is the ifle of Man, and have only a fhore upon one fide. Thefe defcriptions of Ierna, Hibernia, and Iuverna, therefore, decifively appropriate the appellations. It is abfolutely impoffible that the weftern Highlands of Scotland could be meant by them. And it is equally impoffible, that any but Ireland could be meant.

Thus is the firft part of this conclufive argument very eafily overthrown. And the fecond will fall ftill more eafily. It pretends to prove the weftern Highlands of Scotland, the Iar or Iar-in of the prefent Highlanders, to be the Ierna of the antients, and the Scots of thefe Highlands to be native Caledonians, *becaufe* the Scots are called Iar-gael or the weftern Gauls. And, even if we allow Mr. Macpherfon all his premifes, his conclufion is unjuft. Even if we allow Iar-gael to be an original appellation for

R 2 the

the Scots; even if we allow it to mean the western Gael, in opposition to the Picts, the eastern; yet it will not follow, that the Scots were equally Caledonians with the Picts. It would only serve to prove them equally Gael with them. And Mr. Macpherson has repeatedly assured us before, that the Irish equally retain the denomination of Gael with the Highlanders. And I have repeatedly shewn the name to have been common to all the tribes of this island.

Thus inconclusive and illogical is the whole of this argument. The assertion, that the Ierna, Iuverna, and Hibernia of the antients meant, not Ireland, but the western Highlands of Scotland, has been effectually disproved by a reference to the accounts of the antients themselves. And the reasoning from the name of Argyle has been shewn to be founded upon an obvious fallacy, the substitution of one term for another, Gael for Caledon. And the whole turn and complexion of the argument is evidently arbitrary and despotical; asserting Ierna &c. to mean the western Highlands, without any deductions of reason, and merely because these are called Iar at present; and alledging the name of Iargael as a demonstrative evidence of the Caledonian origin of the Scots, without any specification of proofs, and merely because the Scots and the Caledonians were equally denominated Gael.

And

And to this clear refutation of Mr. Macpherson's argument let me add two observations, in order to collect his reasonings on this subject, in different parts of his work, into one point of view.—Hibernia is here without hesitation derived from the Welsh Yverdhon. But in p. 56, 57 we are told, that *it is more probable* it was *not* derived from Yverdhon, and that *we may conclude* it was derived from the Latin Hibernus.—And Mr. Macpherson here argues, that Ierna, Iuverna, and Hibernia, among the antients, as derived from the British Iar-in, Erin, or Yverdhon, must certainly mean the western Highlands of Scotland; when in p. 55 he says expressly, that Ireland was called Iar-in by the Caledonians, and even " in contradistinction" to the western shore of Caledonia; when in p. 56— 57, 62, 63, 81, 94, 95, and 106, he expressly quotes Cæsar, Mela, Solinus, and Tacitus, as applying Hibernia to Ireland; and when in p. 56 he specifies Iuverna, Ierna, Iris, Ουερνια, and Hibernia, as " various names by which the " Greeks and Romans distinguished" the isle of Ireland.—So grossly inattentive is Mr. Macpherson even to his own reasonings before!

P. 131. " In the neighbourhood of Drumal-
" bin, a ridge of hills which divided the Scottish
" from

"from the Pictish dominions, there is a lake, "which, to this day, is called Erin. The river "Erin or Ern rises from that lake, and gives its "name to a very considerable division of the "county of Perth. In this district there are to "be seen several Roman camps to this day. "The Romans could not be strangers to the "name of a country where their armies remained "long enough to leave such lasting memorials of "themselves behind. Juvenal, from the soldiers "of Agricola, might have heard of the district of "Erin, which he softened into Juverna; and "the troops of Theodosius might have carried the "same intelligence to Claudian."

This is the third conclusive argument against the Hibernian extraction of the Scots. And it is full of errors.

The first amounted merely to a possibility. The second assumed the air of certainty and decisiveness. And the third relapses to a mere possibility again. " Juvenal, from the soldiers of Agricola, " *might* have heard of the district of Erin —; " and the troops of Theodosius *might* have carried the same intelligence to Claudian." This is surely a strange mode of reasoning; *possible* in the outset, *certain* in the progress, and *possible* again at the close; like a ninepin, great in the middle, and small at the extremities.

But

But it is still more remarkable, that the third argument directly contradicts the second. In the second, Juverna and Ierna, particularly, are insisted upon to have been applied by the Greeks and Romans to the western Highlands of Scotland. But, in this, the names are supposed to be derived to the Romans from Strathern in the county of Perth, and to have been applied to it by Juvenal and Claudian. In p. 56 the author assigns the names to Ireland. In p. 130 he fixes them upon the western Highlands. And in p. 131 he cedes them to a part of the eastern. We have been so much accustomed to contradictions in Mr. Macpherson, from the clashing parts of his ill-composed system, that we shall the less wonder at the strangeness of this last; and shall be the less surprized to find, that in the progress of his conclusive arguments, and within the compass of a few lines only, he should thus grossly oppose his own sentiments, and wantonly overthrow the edifice which he had been so busily raising.

Many notions in Mr. Macpherson's Dissertation are derived from the writers before him on the same subject. And the substitution of Strathern for the Ierne of Claudian and the Juverna of Juvenal, is particularly made by Sir George Mackenzie

kenzie and Sir Robert Sibbald [1]. But the opinion is a very wild one. Juvenal says:

> Arma quid ultra
> Littora Juvernæ promovimus, et modò captas
> Orcadas, et minimâ contentos nocte Britannos?

Claudian says thus :

> Totam cum Scotus Iernam
> Movit —,

And,

> Scotorum cumulos flevit glacialis Ierne.

And Mr. Macpherson supposes the soldiers of Agricola to have carried the name of Juverna to the one, and the soldiers of Theodosius the appellation of Ierna to the other. But both Mr. Macpherson and his two originals have forgotten, that the name of Juverna is not first noticed by Juvenal, or the name of Ierna by Claudian. Mr. Macpherson himself, particularly, quotes Mela in p. 57, as using the name of Juverna. And I have already shewn Ierna to have been used ages before the days of Claudian. Both were the

---

[1] Sir George in p. 375, and Sir Robert in Gibson's Camden, c. 1490—1497. Edit. 1722.

common appellations of Ireland, when the little
diſtrict of Strathern was buried in the obſcurity
of its own inſignificance. And Erin and its re-
latives being merely denominations of Ireland
derived from its weſterly ſituation, any inſular or
peninſular diſtrict in Britain might receive the
ſame appellation from the inhabitants to the Eaſt
of it. Thus we have Britons and Brigantes upon the
Continent and in Albion. Thus Ireland was called
Inis Alga, and a cherſoneſus in Caledonia Elg-in.
And thus we have the little iſland of Era or Erra
near the iſle of Mull and to the Weſt of it, and
the iſland of Era or Erin near the Harris[1]; Erin
for the whole body of the Hebrides; Ierna on
the weſtern ſide of Loch Fyn in Argyle, and Iernus on the weſtern ſide of Ireland; and Hierna
in the days of the Romans, and two Erns and
two Stratherns at preſent, even upon the eaſtern
ſide of Caledonia[2].

---

[1] See Irwin's Hiſt. Scot. Nomenclatura Latino-Vernacula, 1682, p. 71.

[2] See the Roman ſtation, ad Hiernam, in Richard, Iter 9. And ſee Buchanan, p. 39. vol. i. Ruddiman, for an Ern in Murray, and an Ierna along it, and Ptolemy for the river Iernus in Ireland.

THESE

These are Mr. Macpherson's three conclusive arguments. And surely without any aggravation it may be truly said of them, that they are vague, contradictory, and weak, the unmeaning effusions of a vivacity, that is perpetually catching at the objects which the imagination presents before it, but finds them all illusive in the grasp, and merely bubbles blown up by the breath of prejudice and passion. Mr. Macpherson therefore, like a man dissatisfied with his own conclusions, still quivers about the point, and still adds only to his own embarrassment. After his three conclusive arguments, his doctrine wants new arguments to support it. And these he gives us in the five following pages.

P. 132. " In vain has Stillingfleet observed,
" that there must have been a sea between Britain
" and the Ierna of Claudian.

" Totam cum Scottus Iernam
" Movit, et infesto spumavit remige Tethys.

" Tethys, or the Ocean, it has been already
" shewn, was rather agitated into a foam by
" Saxon, than by Scottish rowers. But, not to
" insist

" infift upon that criticifm, if by Ierna we are
" to underftand I A R, the weftern divifion of
" Caledonia, from Glotta to Tarvifium, the
" many extenfive arms of the fea, which indent
" that coaft, will, at once, remove the learned
" prelate's objection. Should we fuppofe that
" Iar-in, or the weftern iflands of Scotland, were
" the Ierna of Claudian, the objection will al-
" together vanifh, as many of thefe iflands are
" at a much greater diftance than Ireland itfelf
" from the continent of Caledonia. (Stilling-
" fleet remarks, that if Strathern, in the county
" of Perth, fhould be admitted to be the Ierna of
" Claudian, it would be ridiculous in the poet to
" fay, that *the Scots put in motion the whole of a
" small* diftrict of their country. The bifhop did
" not recollect, that it was very common with the
" antient poets to put a part of a country for the
" whole. Latium is often ufed for the Roman
" empire; Mycænæ for all the ftates of Greece;
" and Thule, by Claudian himfelf, for North-
" Britain.

" Quem littus aduftæ
" Horrefcit Libyæ et ratibus impervia Thule.).''

This argument, taking in the whole of what is faid in the note as well as in the text, is founded merely upon fuppofitions, one implied, and

and the other two confessed and acknowledged to be such. " It was very common with the " antient poets," says Mr. Macpherson, " to put " a part of a country for the whole." And it is thence implied that this *may* be the case with Claudian here. And " *if* by Ierna we are to " understand — the western division of Caledo- " nia, &c.; *should we suppose* that Iar-in, or the " western islands of Scotland, were the Ierna of " Claudian, &c." And an argument of an hypothetical nature can plainly be of no service against a positive objection.—But let us descend to particulars.

Mr. Macpherson says, that " *he has already shewn* " Tethys to be agitated into a foam by Saxon " rather than Scottish rowers." He has *shewn* it, as he has *shewn* the truth of too many positions in his work. He has *affirmed* it. His *demonstration* is in p. 114, and runs thus; " We may " safely *affirm*, that the Tethys of Claudian was " rather agitated into a foam by Saxon than by " Hibernian oars."

If we will but allow our author to suppose three things, he will entirely overthrow bishop Stillingfleet's objection. Give me but a footing in another sphere, says our historical Archimedes, and I will shake this at pleasure. And yet, even if we allow him his suppositions and his footing, the prelate's argument and the globe will remain

equally

equally unhinged. — Should we suppose with Mr. Macpherson, that Claudian puts a part for the whole when he speaks of Ierna [1]; neither Strathern, nor any other part of Caledonia, can be allowed to claim the appellation of Ierna. Claudian says,

> Incaluit Pictorum sanguine Thule,
> Scotorum cumulos flevit glacialis Ierne.

Here Ierne cannot mean any part of Caledonia, and be poetically put for the whole of it; because Caledonia itself is mentioned immediately before, as Mr. Macpherson here acknowledges it to be in another place, under the name of Thule. And the Ierna of one passage, and the Ierne of the other, are undoubtedly the same country.— Should the Ierne of Claudian be supposed to mean all the western division of Caledonia, the extensive arms of the sea upon that coast can never come up to the Tethys of Claudian. Or should Ierne be even supposed to mean the western isles of Caledonia, even the sea betwixt them and Caledonia can never comport with the Tethys of the poet. They obviously cannot, in the plain unwrested signification of the word, Tethys or Ocean. And they undoubtedly cannot, according to Mr. Macpherson himself. According to him, Tethys is too great a name to be applied even to the whole wide sea betwixt Ireland and Caledonia. "Tethys signi-

[1] This argument is equally urged by Sir G. Mackenzie, p. 410.

"fies

"fies Ocean: the sea betwixt Germany and England has some right to that title, but the channel between Ireland and Caledonia was never dignified with so high a name" (p. 115). And must not the name, then, be equally too high for the channel betwixt Caledonia and its isles? And must it not be infinitely too high for the mere bays and lochs, that insinuate themselvs into the land along one side of the channel?

But this is not the only contradiction, in which the present has involved Mr. Macpherson. He is now so entangled in the curious web which he is constructing, that, at every motion to expedite and finish the work, he is breaking some principal thread, and letting in destruction upon the whole. He has here advanced three suppositions, That the Ierna of Claudian means the western isles, That it means the western Highlands, and that it means Strathern. These are obviously incompatible one with another. And the contradictoriness of the suppositions is a great addition to the impropriety of them [1].—When Mr. Macpherson supposes the western isles or Highlands to be meant by Ierna, he interprets Claudian literally, as placing the whole for the whole. But when he supposes Strathern to be meant, he interprets him figuratively, and makes a part

[1] So Sir George Mackenzie makes Ierna to be Strathern in p. 375, and in p. 410 all the northern Highlands as far as Invernefs.

to stand for the whole.—When he fixes Ierna to the western isles, Tethys signifies the broken sea, that is crouded with islands, betwixt them and the continent of Caledonia. When he fixes it to the western Highlands, Tethys imports only a few bays and lochs. And when he fixes it at Strathern and interprets it Caledonia, Tethys must obviously import the Friths of Forth and Clyde.—And, to crown all, the author, in his reference to what he *had shewn* before concerning Tethys, has actually remitted us, in confirmation of a part, to a preceding passage of his own, that has not shewn any thing, and that directly contradicts the whole of it.

P. 133. " To collect the whole argument on
" this head into one point of view: The Scots
" of Britain lived in a cold climate; their country
" was situated to the West of such neighbours,
" as had an immediate communication with the
" Romans. The Irish lay under the same dis-
" advantage of unfriendly seasons; and their
" island was similarly situated. The historians
" and poets of the Empire, and the Geographers
" of Greece and Rome, exaggerated—the seve-
" rity of the climate under which both the Scottish
" nations lived. From an exact conformity of
" Genius,

" Genius, language, manners, drefs, fituation,
" and climate, the Scots of both ifles had a
" much better title to the common appellation
" of Hiberni, than Italy, Spain, and a confider-
" able part of Africa, had to the name of Hef-
" peria '."

We may judge of the whole argument from this, Mr. Macpherfon's, account of it. And no author can defire a fairer treatment, than to be tried by his own reprefentations of his own arguments.

Mr. Macpherfon has here jumbled together the two etymons of Hibernia, which he had given us feparately before. We have been told in p. 56 and 57, that Hibernia is " more pro-
" bably" derived from the Latin Hybernus than the Britifh Yverdhon, and that " we may con-
" clude" it to be formed from Hybernus. Notwithftanding this, in p. 130 we have it directly deduced from Yverdhon. And here, in p. 133, we have it derived from both together. " The

---

[1] So Dr. Abercromby in his Martial Atchievements of the Scots fays—" There was a period of time, wherein the Scots " in Ireland and thofe in Britain were by foreigners, who " obferved them both to fpeak the fame language, wear the " fame fort of garments, and follow much the fame cuftoms, " almoft indifferently called Scots and Hiberni" (p. 10. V. I.). — And Dr. Macpherfon p. 96. argues, that the Irifh muft have been Caledonians from a " perfect fimiliarity of ge-
" nius, language, arms, drefs, manners, and cuftoms," between them.

" Scots

"Scots of Britain *lived in a cold climate*—:
"the Irish *lay under the same disadvantages of*
"*unfriendly seasons.*— The historians and poets
"of the Empire, and the Geographers of
"Greece and Rome, exaggerated — *the severity*
"*of the climate* under which both the Scottish
"nations lived. From an exact conformity of—
"*climate,* the Scots of both the isles had a
"title to the appellation of Hiberni." This
is a plain deduction of the name of Hibernia from
the Latin Hibernus. And this derivation is
embraced in p. 56, 57, is rejected in p. 130,
and is embraced again in p. 133. But it is here
embraced along with the other. "The Scots
"of Britain lived in a cold climate: their *country*
"*was situated to the West* of such neighbours
"as had an immediate communication with the
"Romans. The Irish lay under the same dis-
"advantages of unfriendly seasons, and *their*
"*island was similarly situated.*— From an exact
"conformity of *situation* and climate, the Scots
"of both the isles had a much better title to the
"appellation of Hiberni, than Italy, Spain, and
"a considerable part of Africa, had to the name
"of Hesperia [or the West]." This is a plain
deduction of the name from the British Yverdhon. That derivation is embraced in p. 130,
is rejected in p. 56, 57, and is here embraced
again. And thus both, having been alternately
embraced and rejected, rejected and embraced,

S   are

are at last united in friendship together. But the union must be dissolved. The name of Hibernia may perhaps be derived from either the one or the other. But it cannot possibly be deduced from both.

Having thus answered the main substance of the argument, let us pick up some of the subordinate mistakes in it.—The Caledonian Scots and the Irish are said to have had a title to the Latin name of Hiberni, from the coldness of their climate. But must not the Caledonians themselves, as living in the very same country with the former, have been equally entitled to the same appellation?—The Caledonian Scots and the Irish are said to have had a right to the British name of Yverdhon, from their westerly situation. But must not the other Caledonians, the tribes that lived equally along the western shore, in Ross and Strathnavern, have had equally a right to the same denomination?—The Caledonian Scots and the Irish are said to have been called Yverdhon, because they were " situated " to the West of such neighbours as had an " immediate communication with the Romans." But is this true concerning the former? If they resided in Braidalbin, Cantyre, Knapdale, and Lorn, as Mr. Macpherson insinuates in p. 128, they lived more to the North than to the West of all the Britons of western Valentia; and if they were settled only in Argyle, Lorn, and Lochaber,

Lochaber, which feems to be the real truth [1], they were certainly to the North of them all. But if they lived in Strathern only, as Mr. Macpherfon intimates that they did in p. 131 and 133, then they were certainly to the Eaft and the North of the great bodies both of the Caledonian and the Roman Britons. And, even if the Caledonian and the Irifh Scots had been placed to the Weft, would this be a competent reafon for appropriating the name of Yverdhon to them? Muft not all the Britons, from the mouth of the Cluyd to the French channel, have been equally with either entitled to the name of Yverdhon? For were they not at all, at leaft equally, fituated " to the Weft of fuch neigh- " bours as had an immediate communication with " the Romans?" And does not the name of Hibernia appear long before the Romans had any fettlement in the ifland? Mr. Macpherfon in p. 56 acknowledges that it does, affirming Cæfar to be the firft that mentions the name.—The Caledonian and the Irifh Scots are faid to have had a title to the name of Hiberni, " from an " exact conformity of *genius, language, manners,* " and *drefs,*" as well as fituation and climate. But muft not almoft all the other Britons, all that were in any of the northern and mediterranean regions of the ifland, have been equally

---

[1] Bede fixes them on the northern fide of the Clyde.

entitled

entitled to the same appellation, as they were equally conformable in all?

Thus have I gone through the several parts of this collective proof. And I have dwelt the longer upon it, as it is Mr. Macpherson's own account of his own greatest argument; in order to shew it to him in its true colours, unthinking, inconsistent, and trifling.

VII.

FROM p. 137 to 141 Mr. Macpherson is employed in tracing the rise and progress of the fiction, the migration of the Irish into Caledonia; before he has been able to prove it one, and when even afterwards he formally endeavours to prove it. *All* his proofs should certainly have come first. And his history of the fiction should have followed at the close of the whole.

From p. 141 to 146 Mr. Macpherson is engaged in producing some negative arguments, as he himself calls them, in favour of his own doctrine. But as in p. 146 he proceeds to his positive reasons, it is not worth the while to stay and attack the negative. A wise enemy will not blunt his sword in the slaughter of the Velites, when the Legionaries are advancing to the charge against him.

Mr. Macpherson boastingly professes in p. 137 to " conclude for ever the controversy by argu-
" ments, which, though obvious, are new and
" decisive." And in p. 146 he triumphantly threatens, by collecting into one point of view the most striking of Dr. Macpherson's arguments, and adding some observations of his own to them,
" to quash for ever a system which has been so
" long imposed for truth upon the world."

P. 146. " Alba or Albin, it has been already
" observed, was the first name given to this
" island by the Gael, who transmigrated from
" Belgium into the more elevated country of
" Britain. Hence proceeded the Albion of the
" Greeks, and the Albium of the Roman lan-
" guage.

" guage [1].— The antient Scots, in all the ages
" to which our information extends, agreed in
" calling Scotland Alba or Albania. The
" Highlanders and the inhabitants of the He-
" brides have, to this day, no other name but
" Alba for Scotland, and they invariably call
" themselves Albanich, or Genuine Britons. The
" uninterrupted use of this national appellation,
" from the earliest account we have of their his-
" tory, furnishes a moral demonstration, that
" they are the true descendants of the first inha-
" bitants of Britain. Had they been of Irish
" extraction, they and their ancestors would have
" undoubtedly assumed a name more suitable to
" their origin [2]."

The custom of the Highlanders, in constantly calling their country Alba or Alban, and in denominating themselves Albanich, is here esteemed a moral demonstration of their descent from the first inhabitants of the island, who called it Albion. But it is obviously no demonstration of such a descent at all. For, even supposing the first inhabitants of Albion to have distinguished them-

---

[1] Albium is a word unknown to the Romans, and is merely Buchanan's arbitrary translation of the Greek Albion. See his History.

[2] So Sir G. Mackenzie derives the name Albanech from the original name of the island, Albion, p. 387. And so Dr. Macpherson, p. 116.

selves

felves by the name of Albanich, the prefervation of the name by the Highlanders would prove no more their particular and peculiar defcent from the firſt inhabitants; than the retention of the name of Britons by the Strathclydenfes, in the eighth and ninth ages, would prove them the appropriated remains of the Britanni, to the excluſion of the Gallowefe, the Welſh, and the Corniſh; or than the adherence of the name of Brigantes to the Britons of Yorkſhire and Durham, in a much earlier period, evinced them alone to be the progeny of the true Brigantes. The Celtæ of one third of Gaul were peculiarly denominated Galli, and the Galli of one third of Celtica were diſtinctively denominated Celtæ [1]; and yet neither the Galli nor the Celtæ were peculiarly and diſtinctively the defcendants of thofe Galli, or thofe Celtæ, who originally poffeffed themfelves of France. The general appellation of a nation, as I have remarked above, was frequently retained for the defignation of fome particular tribes in it.

But the names of Alban and Albanich, for the country and inhabitants of the Highlands, have no relation at all to the firſt coloniſts of Britain. Thefe I have already ſhewn to have been denominated Britons, Brigantes, or the feparated men. And the fame name, which is

[1] Cæfar, p. 1.

now the general appellation of the whole Highlands, was formerly, and is still, the discriminative name of a part only. In the History of Manchester I have shewn a tribe of the Caledonians to have been called Albanii, and to have inhabited a part of Athol, Braidalbin, Strathern, and Menteith [1]. And Braid-Albin remains to this day the appropriate appellation of a district in the Highlands. Were the Albanii therefore, or are the inhabitants of Braidalbin, peculiarly derived from the first inhabitants? And a long range of country, that ran in a narrow slip from Derbyshire into Scotland, I have shewn to have been distinguished by the name of Alps, a denomination exactly the same as Alba or Alb-an [2]. Was all the country adjoining to this, therefore, in a particular and specific manner peopled by the descendants of the first colony? If they were, what becomes of the exclusive right of the Caledonians to this descent? And, if they were not, what becomes of the argument from Alba and Alban? These words indeed have as little reference to the first colony, as to the inhabitants of the moon. The preservation of the name of Alp or Alb, in so many parts of the island, shews the island and those parts of it to have been denominated from one common principle of

[1] History of Manchester, p. 410.
[2] History of Manchester, p. 140.

sameness,

sameness. Albion, according to Mr. Macpherson himself in p. 39, signifies the High Land, and in reality imports the Heights. Hence it became the natural designation of that part of our island, which must have been seen from the continent, before any of it was inhabited: and what had for ages been the name of all that was seen, as naturally remained the appellation of all of it afterwards. Hence it was the name of the Albanii of Vespasiana, who lived in the peculiarly mountainous parts of the most mountainous regions of Caledonia. Hence it was affixed formerly to the long ridge of hills that runs from Derbyshire into Scotland, and remains affixed to the wild hills of Braidalbin at present. And hence the Highlanders in general to this day distinguish their country by the title of Alba or Alb-an, High Land or High Lands, and denominate themselves the Alban-ich or Highlanders.

But it is very observable in the conduct and direction of Mr. Macpherson's argument here, that, even if every thing was true as it is stated by Mr. Macpherson himself, the point proposed would not be proved at all. The question betwixt Mr. Macpherson and his antagonists is not, whether the whole body of the antient Caledonians or present Highlanders be derived from Ireland, but whether a body of Irish did not come over

over into Caledonia, and communicate their own name of Scots to the Caledonians. Mr. Macpherson, however, has taken the former queſtion for the latter, and argues from that. Not attempting to prove, that no Iriſh paſſed over into the Highlands, and communicated their own name of Scot to the Highlanders, he endeavours to prove only, that the Highlanders do not now acknowledge any Iriſh appellation for their own. This, we ſee, is foreign to his purpoſe. The Highlanders may not do it, and yet may have been conquered by the Iriſh Scots, and may therefore be denominated Scots by others. The Welſh do not acknowledge the appellation of Engliſh, though they have been conquered by the Engliſh, and are therefore reputed as Engliſh in every nation abroad. And the Saxons of all Valentia, being now reduced under the dominion of the Scots, are regularly conſidered as Scots even among their brethren of England.

And there is ſtill another remark to be made upon this argument, which evinces ſtill more the great want of preciſion and diſtinctneſs in Mr. Macpherſon's ideas and reaſonings.—Even if the Highlanders had been peculiarly denominated Albanich or Albanii, even if this had proved them the peculiar progeny of the firſt coloniſts of Britain, and even if the queſtion had been, whether the whole body of the Caledonians was

derived

derived from the Irish; all these concessions would not have enabled the argument, to prove the Highlanders not descended from the Irish. The Highlanders, on this allowance, having been denominated Albanich from their peculiar ancestors, the first colonists of the island; but being at the same time, according to Mr. Macpherson, the actual progenitors of the Irish; the Irish must have been the progeny of the first colonists, equally with the Highlanders. And Mr. Macpherson, with a strange inconsistency, even acknowledges in p. 39, that the Irish retain the name of Alba or Albin equally with the Caledonians, as the name of the Highlands, to the present period [1].

Such is the first of those arguments which are said to be "equally new and decisive," which are "to conclude for ever the conttroversy," and "to quash for ever" the Irish extraction of the Scots. And, if the rest be like this, we may safely affirm, that they will not prove *very* decisive, the controversy will not be *absolutely* concluded, and the Irish extraction of the Scots will not be *totally* quashed.

---

[1] "The Scottish and *Irish* Gael have brought down the "name of Alba or Albin to the present day."

P. 147.

P. 147. "The Belgic nations, who tranfmigrated into South Britain before the defcent of
Julius Cæfar, retained the name of thofe communities on the continent from which they
refpectively derived their blood. The auxiliaries of Vortigern preferved long their original
name of Saxons, and the Scots who fpeak the
Galic language have no other name for England or its inhabitants than Saffon and Saffon-
ich. But if the antient Scots have preferved
among them the true name of the Englifh, for
fo many ages after it had been difufed by that
nation itfelf, it is much more likely that they
muft have retained their own indigenous
name¹."

This is alfo one of the "decifive" and "conclufive" arguments, that are to "quafh for ever"
the Irifh derivation of the Scots. And in the
margin it is called the "fecond proof." But in
the clofe of this argument, when Mr. Macpherfon deduces his inference from it, it amounts,
according to his own reprefentation, to a mere
likelihood or probability. — We are told in proof
the firft, that the ufe of the name of Alba and

¹ So Sir George Mackenzie derives Albanach from Albion, becaufe the Highlanders call the Englifh Saffenach, p. 387.

Albanich

Albanich among the Highlanders, for their country and themselves, is *a moral demonstration* of their peculiar descent from the first inhabitants of the island. And in proof the second, where the same argument is pursued, and should therefore be carried farther, we find it only a *likelihood*, not even that the Highlanders are descended from the first colonists, but only that their names of Alba and Albanich were the original appellations of the country and the people. This second proof against the Irish extraction of the Scots, is therefore no proof at all against that, but merely an argument of probability in favour of the antiquity and primitiveness of the name of Alba or Alban for the Highlands. It is not a new or second argument in itself, but merely the buttress of a former one.— And from both it appears, that the appellation, the use of which by the Highlanders, as transmitted to them from their earliest ancestors, furnished *a moral demonstration* of their derivation from the first colonists, has in itself only a *likelihood* of being their original name.

But let us consider the reasoning by itself, as detached from the previous or subsequent arguments, and as only a probable proof, that the original name of the Caledonians in general was Albanich. Thus considered, the argument at first view carries great probability with it. And I have already shewn, what seems a strong confirmation

firmation of it, that one tribe of the Caledonians was actually denominated Albanii in the days of the Romans. But, when we come to examine it more accurately, even in this light it is incompetent and useless. The inference, that, as the Highlanders have preserved the antient name of the English, Saffon, they have therefore much more probably preserved their own, very reasonable as it certainly is, is directly confronted by a fact. And all inferences of reason, on points like these, must bow down to the paramount authority of facts. The Welsh have equally retained the name of Saffon for the English. And yet they have actually lost their own indigenous name of Welsh. Though this appellation, as I have previously shewn, was even borne by them as late as the sixth century, it is now so totally lost among them, that the criticks have denied them ever to have borne it at all. Thus uncertain is all this sort of argumentation. And thus does the dancing meteor continually elude us, even when we think it most substantial and solid.

The whole body of the Caledonians, however, could never have been, and are not now, denominated Albanich. The name of Caledonia comprizing all that large peninsula of land which lies to the North of the Friths, the appellation of Alb-an, or the mountains, could have been given only to the hilly part of the country, in

oppo-

opposition to the levels of the eastern coast, and the plains immediately to the North of Antoninus's Vallum. The inhabitants of these I have already shewn to have been denominated Mæatæ, or Lowlanders, by the Britons and Romans. And the inhabitants of the hills only are denominated Albanich, or Highlanders, at present. The tribes of the Caledonian Lowlands were denominated Mæatæ formerly, in contradistinction to the nations of the hills. And the clans of the Caledonian mountains are denominated Albanich or Highlanders at present, in opposition to the residents of the Lowlands.

This second " decisive " and " conclusive " argument therefore, as the second, is no argument at all. It is only a part of the first. And, even in itself, it is neither decisive nor conclusive. It pretends only to be a probable proof. And it is not even that. In every view of it, it has been shewn to be grosly defective and erroneous.

P. 147, 148. " Had the Scots been originally
" Irish, *Eirinich* and not *Albanich* would have
" been their proper name. So far were they
" from adopting the name of their neighbours of
" Hibernia, that it is well known that both the
" old

"old Irish and the inhabitants of the North of
"Scotland promiscuously call themselves Gael—.
"The Welsh, in antient times, distinguished the
"Scots of both the British isles by the appellation
"of Gaidhel —, much the same with Gael, in
"the pronunciation. Should then the Scots be
"of Irish extract, it must naturally follow, that
"the Picts sprung from the same source, a doc-
"trine no less absurd than it is new [1]."

I sometimes find a difficulty in discovering the immediate aim and direction of our author's arguments. Very sensible and acute as Mr. Macpherson is, they frequently take their course, like an arrow discharged from a feeble bow, languidly fluttering in their progression, and wadling obliquely towards their mark. And he so confounds the precise terms of the question, that I am obliged frequently to recur to them again.

This, as the margin expressly informs us, is the "third proof" of "the Caledonian extraction "of the British Scots." And this, and the two preceding, have all fallen into the fallacy which I have noted in my remarks on the first. They have all grosly deviated from the point under consideration. Instead of proving, or attempt-

[1] The same argument is in Dr. Macpherson at great length, p. 115—128.

ing to prove, that the Scots did not come over from Ireland, and communicate their own name to the Caledonians; Mr. Macpherfon argues, that the Caledonians themfelves did not come over from Ireland. And in the prefent Extract he confefledly and avowedly falls into the fallacy. " Had the Scots [the prefent Caledonians] been " originally Irifh, Eirinich, and not Albanich, " would have been their proper name." " Should " then the Scots [the prefent Caledonians] be of " Irifh extract, it muft naturally follow, that " the Picts fprung from the fame fource." The delufivenefs of an equivocal term has impofed upon him. And the word Scot is to him what Belgium was before. But the conclufion, concerning the Picts, fhould furely have awakened him from his dream, and fhewn him the wildnefs of his error[1].

This argument therefore is all an Ignoratio Elenchi. And, if every part of it was true, and if the inference from the whole was juft, it would prove nothing concerning " the Caledonian ex- " traction of the Britifh Scots." But neither the premifes nor the conclufion are juft.—If the Caledonians had been originally Irifh, Mr. Macpherfon fays, they would have been called Eiri-

[1] So Sir George Mackenzie goes on in p. 372, 373, 377, 378, 387, &c., arguing with the fame unobferved duplicity of meaning on the word Scot.

nich, and not Albanich. But, as Albanich fignifies only the Mountaineers, fuch of them as refided in the Alban or Heights might, and would naturally, have been denominated Albanich, even if they had come from Ireland. And all the Caledonians, as I have juft fhewn, were not denominated Albanich. Thofe only were fo called that actually refided in the Highlands.—This name of Albanich is principally retained by the weftern Highlanders at prefent[1]. And the name of Eirinich, according to Mr. Macpherfon himfelf, muft have been equally the appellation of thefe Highlanders, as Mr. Macpherfon alledges their country to have been the antient Ierna, and to be actually denominated Eirin by themfelves[2]. The two names, therefore, appear not as the diftinctive and oppofed appellations of two different nations, but are found united together as the joint appellation of the fame people. The national defignation of Eirinich, which Mr. Macpherfon denies to have been ever acknowledged by the Caledonians, appears from himfelf to be actually acknowledged by them. And the name which Mr. Macpherfon confeffes, if it had been found adopted by the Highlanders, would have proved the Irifh extraction even of the Caledonians, is found actually adopted by them, according to his own reprefentation, and even by fuch of them as moft faithfully retain the antient

---

[1] Innes. [2] P. 56 and 130.

appel-

appellation of Albanich. The Caledonians therefore, according to Mr. Macpherson's own assertions, must have been descended from the Irish. And the derivation of the Picts from the same origin, a doctrine which Mr. Macpherson very justly declares to be " as new as it is absurd," appears to be right upon his own reasonings, and to result necessarily from his own principles.

P. 148. " From the name of the district of
" Iar-ghael, which, it has been always said, was
" the first territory possessed by the Hiberno-
" Scottish colony, there arises a very decisive ar-
" gument in favour of our system. Iar-ghael is
" not the name of the country, but of those who
" inhabited it from the earliest times. It signifies
" *the western Gael* in opposition to the *eastern*
" *Gael*, or the Picts, who possessed the shore of
" the German Ocean. But what is conclusive
" against the Irish system is, that Caeldoch, or
" the country of the Gael, which the Romans
" softened into Caledonia, is the only name by
" which the Highlanders distinguish that division
" of Scotland which they themselves possess."

This is called the " fourth proof " against the Irish extraction of the Scots. And it is actually the last. Let us therefore examine it with particular attention. This is intended to leave the whole hypothefis with the ftrongeft impreffion upon the mind. And it is accordingly proclaimed by its author to be " a very decifive argument in " favour of his fyftem," and abfolutely " conclu- " five againft the Irifh."

This is called the " fourth proof." But it obvioufly confifts of two diftinct and feparate proofs. And, as the firft was unwarily broken into two, fo two are combined together in the fourth.

The former of them is called " a very decifive " argument," and is mentioned equally as fuch in p. 130. But it has no weight at all. For, as I have obferved before in anfwer to this very argument, even if we allow Mr. Macpherfon all his premifes, his conclufion will be ftill unjuft. This is wonderful but true. If we allow Iargael to be the name of the original inhabitants of Argyle, and if we allow it to fignify the Scots as the weftern Gael, in oppofition to the Picts as the eaftern; yet what conclufion follows? That the Scots of Argyle were equally Caledonians with the Picts? No, affuredly! It only proves them to be equally denominated Gael with the Picts. And, as Mr. Macpherfon has repeatedly acknowledged even the Irifh to be denominated Gael equally with the Picts, fo have I
shewn

shewn the appellation to have been common to all the tribes of the Britons.

Thus eafily is the force of the firft proof repelled. And the fecond, which claims to be "conclufive," as the other was "decifive," may be anfwered as eafily. It is exactly of the fame genius and fpirit. And, if we allow Mr. Macpherfon all his premifes again, his conclufion will be again unjuft. If we permit him to interpret Caeldoch into the country of the Gael, and if we acknowledge it to be the fame word with the Roman Caledonia, yet no inference will arife from either or both againft the Irifh extraction of the Scots. The only inference is, that the prefent and antient Caledonians were denominated Gael. But it does not prove the Scots to have been native Caledonians, becaufe they refided in the country of Caledonia. The word Caeldoch being the fame with Caledonia, that name can evince the Caledonian extraction of the Scots no more than this. And the whole compafs of the Highlands might be called Caeldoch and Caledonia; and yet the Scots, fettled in a part of the country, might be a colony of people derived from Ireland.

So totally weak and unmeaning is this laft and clofing argument againft the Irifh extraction of the Scots. And the feveral parts of the argument, confidered

confidered merely in themfelves, are equally weak.

There is a wild fpirit of repetition, which colours over the face of Mr. Macpherfon's work. The fame arguments prefent themfelves again and again before us, and frequently in the fame drefs and manner. And this is particularly the cafe with the prefent feries of reafons. All of them have already received their anfwers, and have been difmiffed before. But they are once more returned, and demand a fecond hearing. And, as I have given it to the three preceding arguments, for the fuller elucidation of the hiftory, I cannot refufe it to the fourth and laft.

Mr. Macpherfon afferts the name of Ar-gathel, Iar-gael, or Ar-gyle, to have been the defignation of the Scots as the weftern Gael, in contradiftinction to the Picts, who were the eaftern. But the Scots were not the weftern or the Picts the eaftern Gael, either according to Mr. Macpherfon's former account or the truth. According to Mr. Macpherfon himfelf in p. 131 and 133, the Scots, as inhabitants of Ierna, were feated in Strathern within the county of Perth, upon the eaftern fide of Caledonia, and in the very dominions here attributed to the Picts. But the real country of the Britifh Scots, according to Bede, commenced immediately from the northern margin of the Clyde, and in the prefent region

region of Argyle [1]. And, according to the oldest account that we have after Bede, the diſtrict of Arre-gathel extended not into Roſs [2]. If therefore we limit the region of the Scots by Roſs on the North and the Clyde on the South, it muſt have contained all Argyle, all Lorn, all Lochaber, and the weſtern part of Inverneſs. But, in this poſition of Argathel, the Scots could not poſſibly be denominated the weſtern Gael by the great body of the Caledonians, as they were to the Weſt only of a ſmall part, and were to the North and South of more. And the Picts could ſtill leſs be denominated the eaſtern Gael, as poſſeſſing the eaſtern coaſt. They poſſeſſed not merely " the ſhore of the German Ocean," as Mr. Macpherſon here fixes their poſſeſſions. But, according to Mr. Macpherſon's poſition of the Scots in Strathern before, the Picts muſt have occupied all the weſtern Highlands particularly; and, according to his poſition of his Scots here, along the line of the weſtern Highlands, the Picts muſt have enjoyed all the reſt of the country. The Picts poſſeſſed, in fact, the whole extended compaſs of Caledonia, except Iar-gael, except Lochaber, Lorn, Argyle, and a part of Inverneſs. They reſided therefore to the North and South, as well as to the Eaſt, of the Scots.

[1] Bede, l. i. c. 1. [2] Innes, p. 771.

And the fame people that were firſt denominated Caledonians, and afterwards Picts, were the inhabitants of Caledonia, even when the Romans were actually in poſſeſſion of the eaſtern coaſt. This therefore demonſtrates the name of Iar-gael, Ar-gathel, or Ar-gyle, to have not been deduced from the weſterly poſition of the Scots in Britain. And the ſyſtem, that was raiſed upon the interpretation, is as eaſily deſtroyed as it was ridiculouſly erected. Etymology, the mere menial of hiſtory, is always ridiculous when ſhe throws off her ſubjection, and vainly ſets up for herſelf.

We are farther told, that Caeldoch is the word which the Romans ſoftened into Caledonia, and " the only name by which the Highlanders " diſtinguiſh that diviſion of Scotland which they " themſelves poſſeſs." But this Mr. Macpherſon and I have already ſhewn to be falſe. That Caeldoch is not the only name by which the Highlanders diſtinguiſh their diviſion of Scotland, Mr. Macpherſon has already ſhewn us in p. 38; in which he acquaints us, that " Alba or Albin " [is] the name of [by] which the antient Scots, " in their native language, have, from all an- " tiquity, diſtinguiſhed their own diviſion of Bri- " tain." Nor is this all the contradiction in our author, concerning the indigenous appellations of the Highlands. Here, in p. 148, we are told, that Caeldoch is " the *only* name" for them

among

among the natives. In p. 38 we are affured, that Alba or Albin is equally an indigenous appellation for them. And in p. 146, 147 we are re-affured, that there is " *no other* name but Alba" in ufe for them among the Highlanders. So inattentive is Mr. Macpherfon to his own preceding affertions, and fo forgetful even of the general and vernacular appellations of his own country!— Caeldoch alfo I have proved before to be neither Cael-doch, as Mr. Macpherfon ftates it, nor the fame with Caledonia. Caeldoch I have fhewn to be Caeld-och, and the fame with Gaelt-ach in the Irifh and Galatica and Celtica in Latin. But Caledon I have fhewn to be very different, and equivalent only to the Celtarum of the Romans and the $Γαλατων$ of the Græcians. And Gael, fo repeatedly alledged by Mr. Macpherfon for two contradictory purpofes, to prove the defcent of the Irifh from the Caledonians, and to difprove the Irifh defcent of the Scots, has been repeatedly fhewn to be the common appellation of all the Britons.

But I am tired with refuting the fame arguments over and over again; arguments, that, like the Irifh in the Milefian fables, ftill rife after they have received their death's wound, and challenge their flayers to a fecond combat.

THESE

THESE are the four arguments, which, " though obvious," were faid to be " new and " decifive," and which triumphantly boafted " to " conclude the controverfy for ever," and " to " quafh for ever a fyftem that has been fo long " impofed for truth upon the world." And what have they proved to be upon trial ? The mere ghofts of former arguments, again introduced upon the ftage to furprize and to elevate, and, like true ghofts, pretending to a greater power and authority on their fecond appearance, than they had in their original condition; the formations of fancy, the creations of darknefs, and actually refolving themfelves into nothing at the approach of light.

VIII.

VIII.

MR. Macpherson having thus laboured unsuccessfully in the deduction of the British Scots, it may be expedient for me to investigate their genuine origin. And, as he has endeavoured to make them native Caledonians, I shall endeavour to shew them as they were, the transplanted natives of Ireland. This may now be done with such a decisive weight of evidence, that, if Mr. Macpherson had been apprized of it, he would never, I am convinced, have written his Introduction. And, from that evidence, the true origin and history of the antient Scots has been already given in the History of Manchester. There Mr. Macpherson's objections had been all virtually answered before they were made, and solutions given to his difficulties before they were started. And, as a second and general reply to all his objections and difficulties, I shall here briefly repeat the substance of what I had previously observed upon the subject, reducing it all into one comprehensive view, and confirming it with some additional notices.

When

When the Belgæ, about 350 years before Chrift, croffed the narrow channel into Britain, and fucceffively fubdued all the tribes from Kent to the Land's End; and when, about 250 years afterwards, they invaded feveral of the neighbouring nations; numbers of the Britons took fhipping from the South-weftern fhore of the ifland, and puflied acrofs the fea into Ireland. There the two colonies of fouthern Britons, the only inhabitants of the country, affociated together into one community, under the one appellation of Scoti. Denominated Gael and Britons, from their original appellations in this ifland; they received the defignation of Scoti, as the difcriminative mark of their late emigration from it. The Irifh to this day diftinguifh the Scottifh language by the title of Scot-bhearla, and the Scottifh nation by the name of Kin-Scuit. And Scuite fignifies in the Irifh of the Highlands at prefent, and fignified fo early as the days of Offian, an Emigrant, a Wanderer, or a Refugee[1]. Thefe, the Scots or Refugees of South-Britain, as other colonies fucceffively fettled in Ireland, gradually retired from the margin of the fea, and fpread themfelves in the interiors of the country. By this means, the whole circumference of the coaft being regularly planted with colonies before the days of Ptolemy, the

[1] Hiftory of Manchefter, p. 433, 434.

Scots were entirely cut off from all communication with the shore, and became inclosed within the center of the island. And, thus situated, they necessarily escaped the notice of Ptolemy, who just circles along the shore of the island, and never penetrates, as he penetrates in Britain, into the mediterranean regions of it. The Romans, in the days of Ptolemy, were masters of all the interiors of Britain, but were very naturally unacquainted with the inland division of Ireland. The Romans however, during their long residence of three centuries afterwards in Britain, must certainly have obtained a good general knowledge, at last, even of the midland and central inhabitants of Ireland. And Richard has accordingly transmitted to us some notices, which he collected from them, relative to the origin and the existence of the Scoti there.

But, when the population of the island was compleated, wars commenced betwixt the different tribes. The whole body of the Islanders became engaged in the contest. They divided into two parties. The one consisted of the Belgic nations, and the other of the British. And the latter confederated together, like the Caledonians and the Jews before them, under the denomination of their principal tribe, and received the general appellation of Scots. The war terminated finally about the year 260. The Belgæ were subdued. The vanquished
adopted

adopted the appellation of their conquerors. And all the nations of Ireland were embodied into one Empire, under the general denomination of Scots [1].

At the commencement of thefe wars, a younger fon of the royal family of the Creones in Caledonia, having been fent over with fuccours to the Britons, was chofen their Pendragon by the kings; and the crown was fixed hereditary in his family. And, foon after the conclufion of them, the royal line of the Creones being extinguifhed, their dominions muft necefTarily have devolved to the monarchs of Ireland. This was affuredly the great occafion that firft fettled a colony of the Scots in Caledonia. The occafion indeed is merely conjectural: but it has fuch ftrong coincidencies of reafon and fact in fupport of it, as almoft lend it the fanction of Hiftory. The royal line of Ireland appears decifively from Offian, to have been the younger branch of the houfe of the Creones. This houfe appears as decifively to have finally failed in the perfon of Offian, about the year 320. And in the year 320 we fee a body of Scots detached from Ireland, and fettling in the country of the Creones. The monarch of Ireland would take poffeffion of the devolved kingdom, and would naturally give it as an appenage to one

[1] Hiftory of Manchefter, p. 443—446.

of

of his fons. And in 320 Fergus eftablifhed himfelf in the country, with a body of troops and the authority of a fovereign[1]. Thefe acquifitions of the Scots in Britain were exactly commenfurate with the territories of the Creones, beginning from, or nearly from, the borders of Rofs, and extending to the bank of the Clyde[2]. And the Scots fettled in the country with the abfolute confent of the Caledonians, as appears decifively from the friendly concurrence of both, within only 20 years afterwards, in expeditions into the Roman Province[3]. Nor did they merely fettle there by confent. They muft have taken poffeffion of the Creonian dominions, in confequence of the laws and prefcriptions of the country; as the Creones now affumed a new appellation from them, and were denominated, like them, Ar-gathel, Iar-gael, or Ar-gyle. This name has puzzled all the criticks and hiftorians. But it is nothing more than the IRISH. The Britons being univerfally called Gathel and Gael, fuch of them as went over into Ire-land, Iar-in, or Er-in, muft naturally have received the appellation of Iar-Gael, Er-Gael, Ar-Gael, or the Ir-ifh Britons; and the appellation remains to this day among the Irifh, in their cuftomary appellation for their own language, Caelich

---

[1] Hiftory of Manchefter, p. 444, and 447.
[2] P. 412, and the dimenfions of Argathel before.
[3] Marcellinus, l. xx. c. 1.

Eir-inach,

Eir-inach, or the Ir-ish British. And the colonists of Fergus would as naturally bring it back with them into Britain, retaining the defignation as the note of their peculiar derivation from Ireland. Thefe are fuch remarkable and ftriking coincidencies, with regard to the actuating reafon of that hiftorical fact, the fettlement of the Scots in Caledonia; as perhaps no conjectural reafon ever poffeffed before, and nearly give it all the confidence of attefted truth.

Thus did the refugees of fouthern Britain gradually become the denominators of all the Irish. And thus did they afterwards eftablish a colony upon the eaftern fhore of Caledonia, and in the year 320 firft fix the appellation of Scots within the ifland of Britain. Thence the name was carried gradually, with their poffeffions, over the whole extent of the prefent Scotland. And Hibernians, Caledonians, Roman Britons, and Saxons, have all concurred to form the prefent refpectable nation of the Scots in Britain.

This then is the genuine origin of the Scots, undifguifed by the romantic impertinencies of the Irish fabulifts on the one hand, and undiftorted by the bold fictions of Caledonian prejudice on the other. And at the clofe it is curious to obferve, that the great point which has been fo long agitated betwixt the Irish and the Scotch criticks, and " has for a century and an " half engaged two nations of contending anti-

" quarians

"quarians in war [1]," is now finally determined in favour and disfavour of both. The Irish, and their auxiliaries of England, Lloyd, Stillingfleet, Innes, Carte, and others, who asserted the Cantabrian or Scandinavian descent of the Scots; and such of the Scotch as, in equal opposition to both, strenuously maintained a Caledonian origin for their ancestors; these were all equally and partially mistaken. They who asserted the Cantabrian or Scandinavian descent of the Scots, and were therefore wrong, affirmed likewise their immediate deduction from Ireland into Caledonia, and were therefore right. And they who denied the Cantabrian or Scandinavian origin of the Scots, and were therefore right, denied likewise their immediate deduction from Ireland, and were therefore wrong. The Scots now appear to have been originally Britons of the South, who migrated from the western shore of Britain into Ireland, and afterwards passed from Ireland into Caledonia.—And they who affirmed, and they who denied, the Caledonian extraction of the Irish Scots, affirmed and denied what was equally true and equally false. As the name of Scot was communicated from the South-Britons in the center of Ireland, to all the tribes upon the coast, it comprized the Caledonian nations of the Robogdii, the Venicnii, and the Hardinii. And

---

[1] History of Manchester, p. 450.

the Scots of thefe three tribes, who poffeffed all the North and North-Weft of the ifland, from Fair Head to Balyfhannon, were all original Caledonians [1].—They alfo who affirmed, and they who denied, the Caledonian defcent of the Britifh Scots, affirmed what they could not prove, but what was yet a truth, and denied what all hiftory denied, and what was yet no falfehood. The Scots, that came from Ireland under Fergus, were brought from the country of the Caledonian Robogdii, from the diftrict in the North-weftern parts of Antrim, which was formerly denominated Dalrieta and is now named Route, and were therefore called Dalreudini in the days of Bede, and their country Dalrieta to the 11th century [2]. And the Scots, who have given their own denomination to all Caledonia and all Valentia, were Caledonians that had migrated into Ireland, and that re-migrated into Caledonia afterwards. — Laftly: the Irifh and the Englifh, who affirmed the derivation of the Britifh Scots from Ireland, and referred, as they both conftantly referred, the arrival of thefe Scots to the commencement of the 6th century, affirmed an indubitable fact

---

[1] Hiftory of Manchefter, p. 434, 442, and 443, 444.

[2] Bede, l. i. c. 1, Ufher, p. 320, and Camden, p. 769. And the annals of Tigernach, one of the oldeft hiftories that the Irifh have, affert the Scots of Caledonia to have been derived from Dalrieta in Ireland. Ufher, p. 321.

in the former, but contradicted equally the Roman and the British accounts in the latter, and gave their Scottish antagonists an infinite advantage over them and the truth. The Scots migrated into Britain, and settled in Caledonia, in the year of Christ 320, and were therefore associated with the Picts in expeditions into the Province as early as 340, and have their ravages so frequently mentioned by the Roman and British writers, through a series of 90 or 100 years after it.

This is the true state of the case betwixt these historical disputants. The whole authenticated history of the origin of the Scots, and of their translation to Caledonia, was never yet given without that dubiousness of testimony, which was frequently of equal moment on both sides of the points disputed, without those adherencies of falsehood which disparaged even real and actual truths, and in such a manner as was consistent with every note of time and every incident of history, till it was given in the History of Manchester. And, what is remarkable, this new system of facts is calculated, almost equally with Mr. Macpherson's, to gratify that national pride of the Highlanders, which ought to be moderated, as every other affection of the mind is, but should always be encouraged, as the soul of all the national virtues. The Irish, that were the progenitors of the British Scots, were themselves the descendants of the Caledonians. And, if the Highlanders submitted to the Scots or were reduced by them, they submitted merely to their countrymen, and the Caledonians were reduced by Caledonians. If therefore Mr. Macpherson had entered into this walk of history, he might have equally flattered the prejudices of his countrymen, and have opened a dark and important period of our history. But, unhappily for himself, he took a different direction. Resolving in his own mind to rescue the early part of our annals from " the possession of fiction and " romance [1]," he has unintentionally strengthened the claims of fiction, and has unwittingly endeavoured to add the authority of right to the possessions of usurpation. And he has gone on accumulating one romantic notice upon another, though all history concurred to reclaim him from his error, and though the attestations of history were confirmed by the living testimony of language; the Caledonians, who were reduced by the Scots of Er-in or Ire-land, having-adopted the appellation of their conquerors; the nation and the country being now universally denominated Scots and Scotland; the nation being expressly denominated Hibernia as late as the 11th century, and the people the Irischery as late as

[1] P. 5.

the 14th [1], and their dialect of the British being invariably entitled the Ir-ish or Er-se to the present moment; and the appellations of Scot for the people, and of Erse for the language, being now, in the concurrent usage of all the rest of the islanders, entirely confined and appropriated to the Gael and the Gaelick of the Highlands.

---

[1] Innes, p. 659, and Sir George Mackenzie, p. 390, V. I.— Irwin in his Hist. Scot. Nomenclatura, 1682, p. 6, says, " Our Isle-men and Highlanders are very oft named Hiberni " by strangers—, and *at this day* the English and our Low- " landers call and count them Irish."

I HAVE now gone over the whole extent of Mr. Macpherſon's hiſtorical arguments with regard to the Britiſh hiſtory. And I have gone over it with a minuteneſs of attention and a punctuality of reply, that was ſcarcely ever beſtowed upon a work before. This I owed to the great credit which Mr. Macpherſon has obtained by his diſſertation with the publick, to the high eſteem which I entertain for his abilities and genius, and to the great importance and obſcurity of the hiſtory. Not a ſingle argument in the Introduction, I believe, is omitted in the reply to it. And my anſwers, I hope, have not turned upon little and circumſtantial points, but on the main and eſſential parts of the queſtion. They have not fluttered merely in idle oſtentations of victory over words and ſyllables. And they have not endeavoured to catch Mr. Macpherſon inſidiouſly in the mere eddy of argumentation. I have conſtantly charged him home, I think, upon the great and leading particulars of the queſtion. And when I have done this, when I have ſhewn the inſufficiency of any argument as to its principal end and deſign, I have then endeavoured to point out the ſubordinate miſtakes in it. I have endeavoured to break the phalanx that was particularly oppoſed to me at the time: and, when the rout was begun, I have ſtudied to improve the victory by purſuing the runaways, and by picking up as many of them as I could.

Thefe troops indeed were more formidable in their appearance on the field, than they have been found in the hour of battle. The gaiety of their attire, and the bravery of their afpects, promifed a much greater refiftance than I have met with from them. And I, who entered upon the conteft with a dubious fpirit, and a tremulous exertion of courage, foon warmed with my own fuccefs, and became affured of the victory.

In this, as in the general event of the conteft betwixt Mr. Macpherfon and me, I may have been deceived by that kindling ardour of fpirit, which often anticipates the conqueft it cannot make, or by that delufive felfifhnefs of judgment, which frequently flatters the vanity with vifionary triumphs. But, when I cooly look back upon the progrefs and the conclufion of the debate, I fee no reafon to think myfelf deceived by either the one or the other.

The plan which Mr. Macpherfon had propofed to himfelf, was to prove the exiftence of three diftinct and principal colonies in Britain, to deduce them in an hiftorical manner from the continent, and to point out their refpective operations in the ifland. And, as the firft and earlieft of the three was to be the progenitors of the prefent Highlanders and Scots, fo was it alfo to become the original and principal poffeffors of Ireland. This Mr. Macpherfon fancied agreeable

to

to the fuggeftions of hiftory, to anfwer to the great revolutions in Gaul, and to correfpond with the interior difpofition of Britain. But, to make the real records of both conformable to the demands of this hypothefis, he has ftretched out the hiftory where it was too fhort, he has curtailed it where it was too long, and has given us a narration at laft, with fcarcely a fingle member of that which we ufed to contemplate in the authors of Greece and Rome. And this is executed with fuch a grofs perverfion even of his own quotations, and with fuch plain and manifeft corruptions even of his own authorities, fuch erazings of records, and fuch interpolations of hiftories, as pain me greatly for Mr. Macpherfon's fenfibilities, becaufe they exhibit him in a light, I am fure, the very oppofite of his real character. Mr. Macpherfon, I am perfuaded, is a gentleman of high honour and fpirit, and could not voluntarily have been capable of fuch actions, even in imagination. But what then muft be the magic power of that prejudice, which could thus bind up the force of a difcerning fpirit, and fufpend all his faculties of precifion and judgment; could thus warp his mind from its natural bias of fairnefs, and throw the illiberal hue of difhonefty over one of the moft ingenuous and candid of men! It is furely a melancholy inftance of the weaknefs of the human intellect, even in its

manly

manly exertions of ſtrength. And thoſe only have a right to triumph over Mr. Macpherſon, who are placed in ſome ſphere removed at once from the frailties and the virtues of humanity, who live out of the reach of prejudice and the power of paſſion, who have never felt their minds ſeduced by the enchantments of a new hypotheſis, and have never ſuffered their imaginations to be fired, and their underſtandings to be contracted, by the hot calenture of a patriot ſpirit.

Mr. Macpherſon has aſſerted the exiſtence of three colonies in Britain. But he has proved only one of them to have had any being in it. His Gael, as a diſtinct colony from his Cimbri and his Belgæ, he has nowhere argumentatively deduced into the iſland. And that body of the Britons which is peculiarly the object of the author's attention, and made by him the inhabitants of Caledonia and Ireland, has no real exiſtence in his hiſtory at all. The exiſtence of his Cimbri, alſo, is founded wholly on the ſlight baſis of a verbal criticiſm, the groundwork of the name of Cymri. And, if this would be ſufficient authority for ſuch a capital point in his hiſtory, then might "the pillars of the world be rottenneſs, and "earth's baſe be built on ſtubble [1]." But, what is ſtill more remarkable, the whole even of this

[1] Shakeſpear.

argument

argument is itself established upon a suppofition, and upon a suppofition which is grofsly erroneous, and is not even attempted to be proved, That Cimber fignified, not a native, but a German, Gaul: as the Indian theology founded the world upon the back of an elephant, and planted the elephant itself — upon the back of a tortoife. And the only one of the three colonies, that is proved to have been in the ifland, is the Belgic. Two thirds of the author's hiftorical fyftem are left ungrounded by himfelf. And the third carries fuch a ftrong mixture of falfhood with it, by dividing the Cimbri, or German Celtæ, from the Belgæ, by confounding the original arrival of the Belgæ with the much later defcent of Divitiacus, and by making the Belgæ to prefs the Cimbri beyond the Humber, and to urge the Gael into Ireland, that even this is in effect unproved by Mr. Macpherfon; and the certain truth is dreft up with fuch an accompaniment of falfhood, that we cannot admit it for real hiftory.

This is a juft and fair account of the general ftate of Mr. Macpherfon's work. And, thus defective as he is in the great outline of his Introduction, he has actually filled it up with figures that are all diftorted from their true proportion, and with objects that ought never to have met in the fame piece. The arguments in general are

dark,

dark, inaccurate, indirect, and contradictory. No regular and steady light is diffused through the whole, that, like the dawn of day, gradually increases as it continues, and enlarges as it proceeds, till it is carried at last to a meridian brightness. But, instead of this, a mere twilight prevails over the work, that gives us continually an indistinctness of objects, and just " flings half " an image on the straining eye ;" that, clear in the commencement, is gradually dimmed in the progress, one shade spreading over another, till the objects, that first attracted our attention, successively sink from the sight and are forgotten, and the author at last is nearly losing himself and his reader in the dark.

This is, I believe, as just a representation as can be given, even by the hand of candour itself, of the conduct of Mr. Macpherson in the general prosecution of his arguments. He has all the marks of genius and sensibility about him, but of a genius not tutored in argumentation, and of a sensibility not reduced under the discipline of thought. He thinks strongly, but not regularly. His mind shoots out in vigorous and spirited sallies of sentiment: but it is not accustomed to keep up its vigour, and to maintain its spirit, in a painful deduction of ideas. Blest by nature with the power, but not borrowing from
the

the schools the habit, of thinking, the turn of his argumentation is continually irregular, and the general force of his reasonings is weak and feeble. He is admirably adapted for the brisk essays of a skirmishing war. But he has unwarily entered into a battle, where heavy armour and practised evolutions are sure to gain the day. Not a steadily distinguishing thinker, not a perseveringly accurate reasoner, he is soon confounded with the multiplicity of his own ideas, and seldom sees the object distinctly at which he levels his argument. Spending himself too much in attentions to the colouring of his style, and throwing himself out in a gay irradiation of language, he has no inclination to examine his arguments severely, and he has no power to exert the rigours of corrective criticism upon them; as the birds under the tropicks have their superior gaiety of plumage deducted to them, by the deprivation of almost all the powers of harmony.

From this want of discrimination in his ideas, and from this defect of accuracy in his reasonings, Mr. Macpherson has even fallen into repeated and gross contradictions. And this is the most striking feature in the whole aspect of his work. The inconsistencies of his reasonings are so great, and the oppositions in his quotations, remarks, and incidents are so palpable, that his arguments have been compleatly destroyed before, by

being

being only set in array against each other. The contrariety of parts to parts is so glaring, and this begins so early in the work, and is continued so regularly through it, that in it, as in man, the seeds of death are incorporated with the first elements of life, that they "grow with its "growth and strengthen with its strength," and, on the first occasion that has invited them forth, have burst out, as we have seen, to the absolute destruction of the whole.

It is not the unhappiness of Mr. Macpherson, that he is mistaken in some unimportant circumstances, that he has misrepresented some subordinate facts, and that he has failed in some inconsiderable reasonings. It is not his unhappiness, that he is mistaken in several circumstances of consequence, that he has misrepresented several incidents of importance, and that he has failed in several considerable arguments. And it is not his unhappiness, that he has even failed occasionally, or yet frequently, in main circumstances, in essential incidents, and in arguments of the first magnitude. But it is his singular and unparalleled infelicity, that he has almost regularly failed in all; that scarcely a circumstance, a fact, or a reasoning, however slight and insignificant, is just or apposite; that nearly every important circumstance, every consequential incident, and every essential argument, are either frivolous in their nature or useless in their application; and that

that each capital and leading topic of the work is generally one great chaos of undigested materials, arguments without shape or form, reasonings heterogeneous and repugnant, and darkness brooding over the face of the whole.

This is such a delineation of a work of learning and genius, that my benevolence is hurt, while justice urges my hand to draw it. The portrait is strongly featured. But it is an exact likeness. It is the immediate transcript of the feelings of my own mind. And it is fully justified by the preceding detail of extracts and examinations. Yet, amid the sternest severity of truth, what sort of spirit must that be, which shall not grieve for the author, while it is obliged to reprobate his work? Who will not particularly sigh with me over the fate of a writer, that, possessed of great brilliancy of parts, and furnished with considerable stores of learning, was chiefly unhappy from the selection of his subject? Mr. Macpherson might certainly have played his part with the highest reputation and success, within the circle of truth and incident. But, in a paroxysm of patriot fondness, resolving to heighten into a demonstration what was unable to receive even the colouring of probability, he has fallen in the attempt, as every man in the same circumstances must have fallen. If the antient giants had exerted their singular vigour of body in contests with mere mortals, they must have been as fortunate

tunate as they were ſtrong; but in a triumphant bravery of ſpirits exalting their aims, and attempting to accompliſh what no force could effect, they neceſſarily failed in their efforts, and were cruſhed by the mountains that they vainly wielded, and were buried under the iſlands that they vainly hurled, in a wild hoſtility againſt the ſkies.

THE END.

INDEX.

ARMORICA.

THE varying extent of it formerly, 214, 215; it probably reached along the whole northern and north-western coast of GAUL, 215.
—How far the BRITONS of our island migrated into BRETAGNE in FRANCE, 215, 216; the name of BRETAGNE, not imposed by our islanders, but the antient and original appellation of the country, 216—218; the name of the continental BRITONS derived from the same principle as that of the Insular, 218, 219.

BRITAIN.

It was first peopled from GAUL, and about what time, 29—32:
—Why called ALBION, 91—93.
—Why called BRITAIN, 95—103.
—When the BELGÆ first settled in Britain, and how, and how far they carried their possessions into the island, 63—65, and 69—79.
—BELGÆ and ABORIGINES the only general divisions of the BRITONS, 68, 69.
—The ABORIGINES denominated CIMBRI, and why, 52—55, and 75, 76.
—Both BELGÆ and ABORIGINES denominated BRIGANTES, and why, 71—74, and 98—102.
—Both BELGÆ and ABORIGINES denominated GAEL and WELSH, and why, 76—78, 29, and 122—124.
—Both BELGÆ and ABORIGINES called CALEDONES, and why, 121—124.
—The language of both the same, 83 and 145.
—The manners of both very little different, 83—85.
—Why some BRITONS called SILURES, 89; why some, CANTII, 86, 87; why some, TRINOBANTES, 87, 88; why some, DOBUNI, 88; why some, ORDOVICES, 88, 89; why some MÆATÆ, 136, 137; why some, PICTS, 219.
—The British CURRAGHS very capable of transporting armies across the sea, 178—181.
—The SILURES, masters of the SILLEY isles, 89.

X —The

—The WELSH, why fo called, and when, 76—79; why called CYMRI, 52—55, and 75, 76.

—The interiors of CALEDONIA well known to the Romans, 107—112; the inhabitants of it firſt formed into one Empire, when, 119, 220; why they call themſelves CAELDOCH, 120, 121; why they were called CALEDONES, 121—124.

—WIGHT, iſle of, the ICTIS of DIODORUS, 219.

GAUL.

The firſt migration of the GAULS recorded in hiſtory, 29.

—The GAULS firſt planted BRITAIN, and when, 29—32, 76—78, &c.

—The firſt irruption of the GAULS into ITALY, when, 24, 25; into GERMANY, when, 29.

—Whence the names of GAULS and CELTS were derived, 19-20, 120-121; what they originally ſignified, 122—124; and how GAUL comes now to ſignify a Stranger, 71—74.

GERMANY.

The firſt migration of the GAULS into it, 29.

—The name of CIMBRI never appropriated to the GERMAN CELTÆ, 51—55; how far it extended, and what it originally ſignified, ibid; how it came to ſignify Robbers, 71—74.

—How the name of AMBRONES in GERMANY came to mean Ferocious Perſons, 71—74.

IRELAND.

The IRISH ſtill attached to the wild fictions of their antient Hiſtory, 3.

—The Romans well acquainted with IRELAND, 108.

—When, and by whom, IRELAND was firſt planted, and occupied from end to end, 150—153.

—Why IRELAND was called IRIS, IERNA, IUVERNA, and HIBERNIA, 149; theſe names invariably applied only to IRELAND by the antients, 240—243, and 247—249.

—Whence the IRISH were called SCOTS, 284—286.

ITALY.

—Not firſt inhabited from GAUL, 20.

—The firſt ſettlement of GAULS in it, when, 24, 25.

—The UMBRI not derivatives from GAUL, 20—24; and yet of the ſame ſtock with the GAULS, 24, 25.

MACPHERSON

INDEX. 307

MACPHERSON.

(Dr.)—Author of Critical Diſſertations, one of the two principal writers that have lately endeavoured to invert the order of Hiſtory, by making the SCOTCH the aborigines of CALEDONIA, and the planters of IRELAND, 5, 6; a general character of his work, 6; his knowledge of the CELTIC confined, 86, 141-142, 210, &c.

(Mr.)—Tranſlator of OSSIAN, the other principal writer that has endeavoured to invert all hiſtory, in his Prefaces and Notes to OSSIAN, and in his late INTRODUCTION, 5, 6; a general character of the TRANSLATION and the INTRODUCTION, 6, 7; he plumes himſelf much on his knowledge of the CELTIC, but his acquaintance with it confined, 86, 141-142, and 210.

—*Firſt* general argument in the INTRODUCTION refuted, 11—28; contradictions in it, 15-16, 16-17, 17-18, 27, and 27-28; miſquotation in it, 27; its miſtake in CELTIC, 18—20.

—*Second* general argument refuted, 33—58; contradictions in it, 33-34, 34-35, 38, 43-44, 46, 46-48, and 51; miſquotations in it, 35-36, 38—42, 42—44, 44-45, 46—48, and 56; its miſtake in CELTIC, 51—58.

—*Third* general argument refuted, 58—66; its miſtake in CELTIC, 59—61.

—*Fourth* general argument refuted, 68—105; contradictions in it, 80—82, 80 and 83-84, 90 and 94, 94 again, and 103-104; its miſtakes in CELTIC, 70—74, 85—89, 91—93, and 95—103.

—*Fifth* general argument refuted, 106—153; contradictions in it, 106-107, 106 and 108, 109 and 112, 115-116, 125-126, 129, 134, 136, 139-140, 145, and 148; miſquotation in it, 112-113; its miſtakes in CELTIC, 120-121, 121-124, 130-131, 136-137, and 148-149.

—*Sixth* general argument refuted, 155—293; contradictions in it, 161, 162, 166-167, 178-179, 185, 194-195, 245, 247, 253-254, 254-255, 256-257, 259, 267, 279, 280-281, 281 again; its miſtakes in CELTIC, 209-211, 230—233, 236—238, 263—265, 270-271, and 278—280; miſquotations in it, 230-231, 236-237.

—An exact and minute character of the INTRODUCTION, drawn from the whole, 295—304.

MANCHESTER

INDEX.

MANCHESTER HISTORY.

It has particularly endeavoured to clear up the original annals of CALEDONIA and IRELAND, and to refcue them both from antient fictions and from modern perverfions, 7; its efforts vindicated, and its accounts confirmed, *paffim*.

—Two miftakes in it rectified, 136, and 137.

—It contains the firft authentic hiftory of IRELAND, as to the original population, &c., that has been hitherto publifhed in any language, 153: and the firft clear, certain, and confiftent account of the origin of the SCOTS, and of their derivation into CALEDONIA, 291.

MARCELLINUS

(Ammianus) — a paffage in his hiftory vindicated from the unjuft meaning univerfally put upon it, 237—239.

SCOTLAND.

The genuine SCOTCH, who, 1.

—Thefe have lately recovered themfelves from their attachment to the wild fables of their antient hiftory, 1, 2; but have ftill a ftrong tendency to the fabulous, and from the old principle, 3, 4; and have therefore endeavoured, particularly of late, to drefs up their antient hiftory according to their own fancies and prejudices, 45.

—The IRISH fictions concerning the origin of the SCOTCH, too extravagant to be worth refuting, 155.

—The SPANISH or the SCANDINAVIAN extraction of the SCOTCH, lefs abfurd, but equally falfe, and eafily refutable, 156.

—The SCOTCH are not fettled in North-Britain by Bede, before the commencement of the Chriftian æra, 212, 213.

—Which of the SCOTCH called ALBANICH, and why, 270-271, and 274; which of them called EIRINICH, IRISHERY, &c, and why, 274, and 292, 293.

—ARGYLE, its original extent, 278, 279; why fo called, 287, 288.

—What gave rife to the name of SCOT, 284—286; whence it came into CALEDONIA, and how it covered the whole country, 286—288; the controverfy concerning that origin being now finally adjufted, after it has lafted near two centuries, 288—291.

www.ingramcontent.com/pod-product-compliance
Lightning Source LLC
Chambersburg PA
CBHW022049230426
43672CB00008B/1120